STRONG ON DEFENSE

STRONG ON DEFENSE

Survival Rules to Protect You and Your Family from Crime

Sanford Strong

POCKET BOOKS
New York   London   Toronto   Sydney   Tokyo   Singapore

The techniques and suggestions presented in this book are the result of the Author's experience in working with law enforcement and crime victims. Criminals, particularly violent criminals, are unpredictable and may not react as expected in given situations, and suggested preventive and responsive measures may not be effective in all circumstances. Care should therefore be taken when following the author's suggestions. The Publisher does not warrant or endorse the techniques and methods presented in this book. The Author and the Publisher assume no responsibility for any injury or damage to persons or property which is incurred as a consequence, directly or indirectly, of the use and application of any of the contents of this book.

Article on pages 40–42 reprinted by permission of *The San Diego Union-Tribune*.

 POCKET BOOKS, a division of Simon & Schuster Inc.
1230 Avenue of the Americas, New York, NY 10020

ISBN: 0-671-52293-0

First Pocket Books hardcover printing May 1996

10 9 8 7 6 5 4 3 2 1

POCKET and colophon are registered trademarks of
Simon & Schuster Inc.

Design: Levavi-Levavi

Printed in the U.S.A.

Contents

Foreword   vii

Part I. Random, Senseless, and Explosive   1

What We're Up Against   1
What's Ahead   7
What Doesn't Work   9
     Gadgets   9
     Martial Arts   11
     Women's Self-Defense?   12
     Doing Nothing   14
What Does Work   17

Part II. Dealing with Fear   20

Breaking Through Fear   20
Fight-or-Flight Response   28
Expect to Be Injured   29
Hard-Line Approach   31

Part III. Mind–Setting Against Violence   35

Your New Survival Mind-Set   40
Your New Attitude   46
Deadly Mistakes   49
The Four Survival Rules to Live By   50
     Rule #1: React Immediately   52
     Rule #2: Resist   60
     Rule #3: Crime Scene #2   72
     Rule #4: Never, Never Give Up   82

Contents

Part IV. The Four Rules in Action   91

Intervening in Violent Crimes	91
Armed Robbery of an Open Business	95
Car Crimes	96
Carjacking	110
Bumper Crimes	118
Forced off the Road	122
Stranded	125
Murder in Public Places	136
When Friends Are with You	144
Impersonating Cops	153
Mob Violence	161

Part V. Families Under Attack   163

Home Intruders	170
Teaching Family Survival	180
Teaching Children Crime Escape	182
The Escape-and-Survive Family Drill	187

Part VI. Six Ways to a Safer Future   196

Three Long-Term Ways	197
1. Guns—Five Criteria Before Loading 197	
2. The Cellular Wave 222	
3. Community Policing 225	
Three Immediate Needs	229
1. Guns off the Streets 230	
2. Gangs 234	
3. Recidivists 236	

Epilogue   241

The Facts on the Cost of Crime	241
We're at the Fork in the Road	244

Foreword

We used to be able to prevent crime from happening, even avoid violent crime by "staying away from the bad areas." That's all changed.

Violence in our day is random, explosive, and a hundredfold more senseless than ever before. In fact, violent crime alone has gone up 300 percent since 1964. Worse, sociologists who specialize in crime trends are blunt with their predictions: "In the next ten years, criminals will be younger yet, more ruthless than now. The crime we have experienced thus far will pale in comparison to the crime wave by 2005."

There's a new breed of criminal you, I, and our families now face. He's young, he's armed, he's most likely high, and he has a thumbs-up, thumbs-down attitude toward your life and mine.

These are the facts: If violence strikes, survival depends on what we alone do in the crucial first few seconds. The police won't be there to help. They'll get there later to pick up the pieces. I know, I was a street cop. In the early 1960s, three police officers were available to respond to calls for help for every violent crime committed. Now in some of our large cities, there are ten violent crimes per available cop. To return to our former level of safety, we would have to hire at least thirty-two times as many cops as are currently in uniform throughout America. It won't happen, and it's not the answer. Safety from crime for you and your family is your responsibility. That's why you need to know what cops know about how to survive.

My background is law enforcement. My specialty was teaching cops how to defend themselves—how to survive—and SWAT officers how to use and protect themselves against guns. My approach is tough-minded, direct, and hardline. There are no softhearted rapists or merciful killers out there.

My aim with this book is to teach you how to survive violence based on the principles I taught to cops. No exceptions. Nothing less. You need it that way.

In police and SWAT training academies throughout the United States, the core of officer survival training is the survival mindset. For everyone, any age, anywhere, and under any condition, that means having bottom-line survival decisions made before violence strikes.

The simplest analogy here is a family fire drill; in a life-or-death situation, you must have an escape and survival plan to fall back on . . . a plan decided on in advance. In a raging house fire or exploding violence, a survival mind-set creates a point of reference, a starting block for that moment when the difference between life or death is decisions made immediately.

This is not a crime-prevention book. This is a crime-survival book. Big difference. Prevention is everything you and your family do to reduce the odds of being a crime statistic. It's important. Survival is what to do when the crime is going down and what is instantly done or not done likely decides who lives and who dies.

At crime scenes it was always clear that many victims had given some thought and effort toward crime prevention but nothing to crime survival. This is the void this book fills. It takes you and your family beyond crime prevention to how to make split-second survival decisions. Self-defense gadgets don't cut it. Not even guns work for most people because they can't use them safely and effectively. The advantage of a survival mind-set over everything else is that it's always with you and ready for immediate use. That's crucial and lifesaving because when violence explodes the security of your world, there are no second chances and no time-outs to think it over and decide what to do.

Survival mind-set training began thirty years ago in police academies when for the first time in U.S. history cops became for some in society their focal point for anger and first targets of violence. I was fortunate to be a part of the beginning stages of teaching fellow cops how to survive violence themselves. Today that survival mind-set training has repeatedly proven itself as the key to a cop's surviving violent assaults. Despite the current sky-rocketing of incidents of violence against cops, the number of cops killed or injured has declined since the midseventies by almost 43 percent. The opposite is true for citizens for whom serious injury and death are at an all-time high. In a nutshell, the difference between police and citizen survival rates is mind-set training.

This book will first help you face this fact: if you or a loved one is the target of criminal violence, they will do to you the same as was done to past victims—you're not different, just next. Then, it will lead you and show you how to lead your family to bottom-line survival rules to fall back on when the shock of violence is overwhelming and the paralyzing fear grips you . . . so that you have a chance to change the outcome.

Strong on Defense makes available to men, women, and their families the same survival training provided to law enforcement for this reason: you and your families face those violent bastards before cops do.

Part I

Random, Senseless, and Explosive

WHAT WE'RE UP AGAINST

The Department of Justice advised in 1993, "Without a complete reversal in present crime trends, eight out of ten Americans will be the victim of violence at least once in their lives." In December 1994, the Justice Department updated their advice: "Every American now has a realistic chance of being the victim of violence including murder because of the randomness of today's violence." FYI: twenty years ago in the early seventies that prediction of violence was one in thirty; ten years ago in the early eighties it was one in twelve.

FBI director Louis J. Freeh spoke to all Americans in November 1994 about today's violence: "This nation can finally learn there are no longer any sanctuaries from deadly crimes."

In less than ten years, we're likely to look back on the early nineties and see them as the good ol' days . . . when we had peace. We can stop this madness, but first we and our families must learn the rules of survival.

Violence explodes at unlikely places in our times. "Random violence won't hit me" is a dangerous assumption. Being reasonably cautious—staying out of unsafe or deserted areas, not staying out late at night, never going out alone at night, and having a good home security system, etc.—isn't good enough anymore. These days, it is less and less clear which areas are safe and which aren't. Violent crime no longer happens only to people who use poor judgment.

Vera Wang is an exclusive bridal shop on Madison Avenue, one of Manhattan's most upscale shopping areas. The shop has a receptionist at the door and sells dresses that average $4,000. In March 1994, a couple from Maryland was watching their daughter trying on a wedding gown when two gunmen burst in. The mother was wearing a diamond ring valued at $60,000; the gunmen yanked it off so hard they broke her finger. Then they shot both her and her husband in the stomach. The couple recovered. The gunmen have recently been sentenced.

La Jolla, California, is an upscale seaside resort area. On Mother's Day, 1992, gang members from Los Angeles and Chicago met in La Jolla and split into two teams and simultaneously hit two of the most exclusive jewelers in California, Jessop's and C. J. Charles. They used hammers to smash and break into the display cases; at Jessop's they shot and killed a businessman and father who was purchasing a Mother's Day gift for his wife.

These were wake-up calls for Manhattan's Upper East Side and La Jolla, where few had feared for their safety because of both areas' exclusivity. For many, it was finally proof that there are no safe places.

Experts argue about why violence has increased so rapidly in the past thirty years: society is too soft on criminals; poverty undermines character; movies; television; rock music; some advertisements promote violence and misogyny; rampant drug use. Regardless of whose research you listen to or the title of the "expert," no one knows for certain. However, you and I know this: if violence explodes at us, we won't care about socioeconomic or cultural theories or the failings of the criminal justice system.

Are we Americans paranoid for worrying about crime—for making it one of our number one fears? No. Period.

I remember being a twenty-year-old, paranoid Marine in the mid-sixties. All of us were. Our DI laid it on the line for us: "You're not being paranoid when you worry about people out there who might try to kill ya when there are people out there who are going to try to kill ya." He never sugarcoated anything—instead, he made us face facts. That's what we needed.

Jonathan Oberman, New York City public defender since 1983 and associate clinical professor at the Criminal Law Clinic of Cardozo Law School:

Street crime today is more violent, more random, more irrational, than it was twenty years ago due primarily to the change in the drug of choice from heroin to crack. The chemical nature of the high is different. Heroin downs users for hours, makes them mellow; the quintessential moment of the high is the "nod." When the heroin addict needs money, he generally avoids contact with other people and seeks to commit crimes of property.

In contrast, crack, the burnable form of cocaine, is an intense, more hyper high, more quickly addictive than powdered cocaine. Crack is a cheap, quick hit — a jumbo vial today costs three dollars — but the user turns mean and violent in response to the need to constantly re-up. When the crack addict needs money, he is fearless and crazed in attacking other people for the few dollars needed to re-up.

Not only are individual users affected differently by heroin and crack, but the means of distribution and production are different for heroin and crack. Historically, a limited number of criminal organizations monopolistically controlled heroin distribution and conducted business according to recognized rules, e.g., transgressing borders meant war, by and large fathers weren't killed in front of their children.

Today, anyone with a stove, two saucepans, and an eighth of an ounce of cocaine can set up a crack factory. The result is a debased form of capitalism: cheap production of a product characterized by planned obsolescence and incredible repeat demand: "feed the pipe, hit the pipe." Since anyone on any block can control the neighborhood distribution of crack, the dealer is no longer obligated to a crime organization; his only goal is to stay in business and maximize profits, and he benefits from being more unfeeling than his competitors to protect his turf.

In this environment, the only guiding principles are money and violence. Social controls, rules, shared values, and defined norms of behavior all disappear. The result is a culture of chaos and depravity: no longer is any distinction made between business and nonbusiness, between participants and bystanders, between intention and result. Anybody can and does kill anyone else for any reason.

In thirty-three years, America endured an increase in crime unprecedented in our or any other industrialized country's history: 14.1 million crimes of all types reported in 1994 alone . . . more crimes than the population in many countries.

- From 1960 to 1993, total crime increased over 550 percent.
- From 1960 to 1993, total violent crimes increased 300 percent.
- In 1960, 288,460 violent crimes were reported. In 1993, 1,924,188 were reported.

Those crime percentages and numbers of crimes are total U.S. violent crimes. The following numbers are for murder rates alone during the same period.

- 1960: 9,030 murders in America. 1993: 24,526 murders in America.
- In the four years from 1990 to 1994, over 90,000 Americans were murdered, almost twice as many as were killed during the ten years of the Vietnam War.

The FBI Crime Clock

1973	1993
(first FBI crime clock)	
1 violent crime every 36 seconds	1 violent crime every 16 seconds
1 rape every 10 minutes	1 rape every 5 minutes
So few serious crimes at schools, they were not recorded	1 serious crime every 6 seconds at schools

Note: In 1960, almost all crimes were reported, whereas in 1993, only 30 percent of actual crimes were reported. That's correct, the actual numbers for total crimes in 1993 are three times higher. Remember, in contrast to thirty years ago, reported crimes in our day no longer reflect total crimes.

It's worth your knowing: in 1994, of the 1.85 million *reported* crimes and 755,000 arrests for those crimes, only 154,000 criminals were sent to prison (DOJ). If a 550 percent increase in crimes with 70 percent of crimes unreported is not enough to justify dismay with our justice system and worry for our families, brace for this: police rates for solving crimes are down from almost 91 percent in the sixties to 66 percent in 1993. For your information, there are two reasons why solving today's violence is so difficult:

(1) Fewer witnesses are willing to testify against local gang members. (2) The nineties has ushered in a shift toward random, stranger-to-stranger violence. In the sixties, 93 percent of murders were committed by people known to the victims: siblings, lovers, spouses, friends. As of 1993, for the first time in our history, up to 50 percent of homicides are random/stranger-to-stranger. In plain talk, innocent by-standers killed by warring gangs and crime victims killed by career criminals are at the heart of not only driving up the murders in America but also driving down police arrest rates.

Justified fear? People live in fear for many reasons. Some reasons are irrational and unfounded. But our fear over violence is clear as day. Some wrongly say that our skyrocketing crime rates and levels of fear are fueled by the vicious and lethal use of guns. The facts are, guns are being used to kill—the killers are our skyrocketing numbers of recidivists, America's career criminals.

The root of the crime problem facing us all in our everyday lives are the recidivists. They are the 10 percent of the criminal population responsible for two-thirds to three-quarters of all crime, including violent crime, in the United States (DOJ). If America could have controlled the recidivists (for starters, not release them from prison time and time again), between 70 and 80 percent of the increases in all crimes would not have occurred. That's not a misprint . . . "not have occurred." Because we don't control them, we continue to look down the barrel of their guns. America's criminal justice system gets its lowest marks when dealing with recidivism. Tragically, it's the reason we are subjected to thirty years of wave after wave of increasing crime.

In a nutshell this is how we got into this mess. In 1964 we began an experiment with criminal justice. Our focus shifted from punishment of criminals (prison time) to criminals' rights with early release for rehabilitation and education out of prison. The result is 70 percent recidivism and skyrocketing crime.

The bottom line: If you or a family member are ever confronted by a criminal anywhere, under any condition, count on this: the odds are 70 to 80 percent you're face-to-face with a recidivist. That makes him violent, experienced, hardened. Count on this, too! He has a rap sheet of crimes committed against other innocent people before you; he won't change his history of violence for you—no matter how much you plead, argue, pray, or promise. To a violent criminal, you're not different from those before you, you're just next.

Recidivism affects your and my safety right now. Young gang members, who are or soon will be recidivists, too, will only worsen our society in the future, unless we take what some will call draconian law-enforcement measures fast! I discuss those measures in Part VI.

WHAT'S AHEAD

September 24, 1995, Janet Reno, attorney general, in her straightforward way, said, "Unless we act now to stop young people from choosing a life of crime, the year 2000 will bring levels of violent crime to our cities that far exceed what we've experienced."

President Clinton said on the same day, "Juvenile violence is America's top problem."

"This is the lull before the crime storm. There is a tremendous crime wave coming in the next ten years," says James Fox, criminologist and dean of the College of Criminal Justice at Northeastern University. The next wave will be driven not by old, hardened criminals, but by teenagers who are turning murderous—"the young and the ruthless," in Fox's phrase. "The nation's murderers are becoming younger and younger." The age group of fourteen to seventeen is committing far more of the nation's murders—up 165 percent between 1983 and 1993 alone.

"There has been a pervasive disinvestment in American youth over the last thirty years," he points out. "Negative forces such as drugs, guns, gangs, television, and movies have grown more powerful as the positive forces of family, school, church, and community have grown weaker. Kids are the least deterrable. They don't consider the consequences of their actions, and many of them don't expect to live to be twenty-one years of age. Why would they worry about prison?"

Fox's predictions on the nation's murder rate have been wrong only once, in the 1980s. "I didn't envision crack," he explains.

As a twenty-three-year-old in the police academy in 1966, I was given a warning I didn't believe. We were told by an old-time cop and trainer, "The most dangerous criminals you will confront will be the juveniles. They will be the most likely to kill you as a lark and for nothing. They'll kill over trivial matters and not care about the consequences for a split second." I now know he was right. Of the four times I was hospitalized as a police officer, two times resulted directly from teenage assaults.

I have spent twenty years in law enforcement, and as of 1995, nine years researching criminal justice and law enforcement issues. Since my early twenties, most of my friends have been in law enforcement. When we get together, I can't help noticing how shocked we all are by how dangerous society is becoming, and we're cops! As Americans we used to point to other countries as sites of social disorder and random violence. Now our crime rates are higher than in most countries, industrialized or third world.

WHAT DOESN'T WORK

I want to get these issues out of the way up front. Life would be much easier if we could just prevent crime beforehand or carry some high-tech gadget that works against real criminals as well as they do against the television criminals. Real crime goes down so fast that your only chance is to respond with action that is immediate, direct, and explosive. When you hear of a new crime defense system or product to buy, do a reality check: Is it as simple as it must be to work at real crime scenes? That reality check is critical if the worst happens, because the people behind the promises won't be on hand to help you out or back up their guarantees. Crime protection doesn't require physical toughness or a lot of gadgets, it requires mental preparedness.

Gadgets

Most so-called defense weapons are either worthless gadgets or seldom available to be of any help to you. They (and often real weapons as well) end up in the hands of criminals. Worse, gadgets give a false sense of security.

The two most popular crime-prevention devices available are the Mace/pepper type of chemical spray and the handheld noisemaker. Mace/pepper spray can be effective, but only if you know how to use it properly. That means at the moment of attack, you must already have it in your hand, ready to go, aimed in the right direction. It can't be in your pocket or purse. If you do carry Mace/pepper spray, and if the attacker knocks it from your hand (that happens to more than half the people who try to use a chemical spray), instead of trying to get it back, escape.

Strong on Defense

People use noisemakers for two reasons: to repel attackers and to get others (neighbors, etc.) to call for help upon hearing the noise. First, no noisemaker lives up to its advertising. The San Diego SWAT team bought a $4,000 noisemaker in the late sixties, eight feet in diameter, came with a trailer, guaranteed to produce "piercing levels of noise the human ear cannot withstand." We tried it during riots twice and against a shooter barricaded in a three-story apartment building: the rioters weren't even fazed, the crook didn't give up. Noisemakers do emit loud, piercing noises, but the noise is bothersome only in small, enclosed spaces, whereas crime victims generally carry them for protection out of doors, where the noise is dissipated. Second, our society is so noise- and alarm-cluttered that people seldom even look out the window when they hear alarms outside. Far fewer people call the police when they hear a noise alarm (whistles, car alarms, etc.) than the sellers of these products would like you to believe. In my experience working in police dispatch, it was rare that anyone called to report any alarm. I remember a four-or-five-block, backyard, fence-jumping chase of a rapist that involved yelling, shots fired, and everybody's dog going crazy; the melee resulted in one phone call received by dispatch.

When I was a young police officer, the department issued Mace to everyone. One afternoon I spotted a burglary suspect and chased him down an alley. After hopping a few fences, I caught him against a wall. I could see he was young. I pulled out my Mace and yelled, "Freeze or I'll squirt!" (I regretted that wording immediately.) He didn't freeze. I squeezed off the first spray. Right into my own face. He got away. I was a mess. It must be in your hand, ready to go, pointed in the right direction.

Martial Arts

There's nothing wrong with the martial arts except that as normally instructed, they're not the answer to surviving violence. In their pure form, they have many objectives: discipline, control of both body and mind, as well as mastery of different stances and movements. Crime survival has one objective: to make split-second decisions under the stress of violence and a time of life or death.

Parents ask me if their children should study martial arts. My answer is yes, but not for crime survival. Do it for pride in personal accomplishment, respect for others, ability to concentrate, unsurpassed balance, self-control, and development of self-discipline. It's also a great way for a youngster to experience some physical pain—to learn what it is like to be hit, to be knocked down and get back up, to not give up. But the martial arts, as customarily taught, are not intended and do not work as a crime survival technique.

Experienced martial arts instructors are masters at concentration. To be a master at crime survival, too, they need only to trim all the moves, all the positioning, down to only survival and escape moves. Reducing to utmost simplicity is difficult—adding on is easy. Crime survival training reduced to only that which is necessary to escape is an art.

Officer David Dye has been a member of the Costa Mesa Police Department since 1967. He has been featured and is regularly quoted in all martial arts magazines and on all the major networks. As an eighth-degree black belt who is in the World Martial Arts Hall of Fame, he still runs his own training studio. According to Dye:

"The martial arts take discipline and time—six years to earn a karate black belt, earned with sweat. If you want something fast and easy, martial arts are not for you. The martial arts and crime survival are very different disciplines. Martial arts techniques have been used since the seventeenth and eighteenth centuries. Crime situations today are very different, as are the types of weapons used. A martial arts instructor who also teaches crime survival must bring the traditional forms of martial arts current with what is going on today. Few martial arts teachers have that dual expertise. Effective crime defense needs real-life crime scenarios. Training must be as real and direct as possible so your students will remember it under the stress of an attack.

"The philosophy of my school is to teach both the 'art' side and the 'practical' side, but always to teach them separately. The dojo is a controlled environment, the street is anything but.

"I once attended a martial arts seminar for instructors. The seminar leader brought out a 12-gauge pump shotgun and cranked in a dummy round—nobody realized it was a dummy round. He walked up to a high-ranking black belt from Japan and shoved it in his face. Every black belt in the room froze. That instructor with the shotgun brought a little reality back to the room."

Women's Self-Defense?

Crime protection approaches intended only for women assume they are weak, less capable of defending themselves, and therefore need different methods from men to counteract violence. The fact is, surviving crime requires far more mental toughness than physical abilities. Size, weight, conditioning, and upper-body strength don't make the difference. If they did, a lot of men would be in deep trouble. Crime survival takes tough-minded mental conditioning, the same for both men and women.

Much of women's self-defense is not only ineffectual, but insulting as well. Women have been told to "use keys between your fingers, carry a hat pin or umbrella to jab at him, do something vulgar to gross him out, tell him you have VD." If any of that junk worked, we'd be teaching men to do the same thing.

The following examples of advice still show up in high schools and women's self-defense courses: "Evaluate the rapist . . . try to pick up clues on how to deal with him . . . maintain your emotional stability and you will maintain control." "Do not overreact. Remain calm. Go along with his demands for a short period . . . stall him. This will give you time to devise an escape plan." All of this is unrealistic and not workable at a rape crime scene.

Imagine if the percentages of women and men raped were 50-50 instead of 98 percent women and 2 percent men. Outside of prison, those are the true percentages. Now imagine someone telling men, "Don't overreact to rape, guys. Go along with his demands so you won't be hurt."

Ladylike self-defense, the anticrime gadgets, the martial arts self-defense programs marketed to women, are too often designed to be quick and easy, with unrealistic guarantees. One direct-mail women's safety device provides an "instant and easy self-defense video for women. . . . Can you point? . . . Raise your hand? . . . If your answer is yes, you can instantly escape anything from rape to severe attacks. . . . It's quick and easy." One television commercial for a women's self-defense program promises "two-minute, guaranteed knockout using your feet. When your assailant tries to grab you, drop to the ground. Use the heel of your shoe [while still on your feet, I guess] to strike into his head over and over." I urge you, concentrate only on escape— never on going to the floor or ground to fight back.

Too much of what is taught in women's self-defense courses won't help them against the violent bastards they go up against. Ninety-five percent of all rapists are recidivists. With rare exceptions, you've got no chance to dissuade a rapist with talk, gadgets, or fancy gymnasium moves.

·

Quick and easy appeals to all of us, but I know from experience there's no such thing as quick and easy or a guarantee when violence explodes. If you buy some police radar detector that's guaranteed to work but doesn't, the consequence is a speeding ticket. If you buy a self-defense gadget with guarantees, you stand to lose permanently. Worse, if you accept someone else's worthless guarantee, you'll end up relying on something that will not produce for you and you'll be worse off because you'll have a false sense of security. If any so-called self-defense device promises a "guarantee" or "quick and easy," walk away from it.

This bottom line should be adopted by every woman, every women's self-defense teacher, and every parent of a daughter: If the how-to-survive-violence technique and advice is not acceptable to men, it's not acceptable to women.

Doing Nothing

Doing nothing against a violent attack is the biggest risk of all because it makes resistance and escape later far more difficult. Worse, it increases the likelihood that violence will escalate, especially when the crime is rape. The most profound example in our country involving resisting (doing something) versus submitting (doing nothing) was a Department of Justice study of rape published in 1985.

Countless myths that had long surrounded the issue of rape were shattered with this study, though it was not surprising to law enforcement officers who had had first-hand dealings with the victims.

- Unlike armed robbers and home intruders, rapists do not normally prearm themselves with weapons. Only 23 percent of 1.6 million cases studied involved men armed with knives or guns, with an equal break of 11 percent knives,

12 percent guns. The major exception to this are rapists who break into a residence; 96 percent grab a knife from the kitchen.

- Approximately 51 percent of women resisted in some form, ranging from screaming to fleeing, to fighting back; the remaining 49 percent did nothing.

- Over 96 percent of all the injuries for both women who resisted or did not were abrasions, lacerations; yet, this statistic was not affected by the rapist's wielding a weapon or determined by the victim's resistance, as old myths once declared. When broken down between resistance or submission, there was only an increase of 2 percent in the injury level to the women who resisted.

- Under 4 percent received major injuries that required a prolonged hospital stay; and the majority of those were raped in an isolated area or trapped in a home or apartment.

    Gang rape, protracted torture by one or more foreign objects, all require time while isolated and controlled.

- Only .03 percent were also murdered, the lowest percentage of all violent crimes.

In public or semipublic places—parks, jogging paths, parking lots, etc.—women have a good chance to escape rape with minor physical injuries. But, the resistance must be immediate and forceful. It's not the resistance of the victim that controls the degree of injury, it's the place. This is crucial information for women to understand about resisting rape: when and how! And especially important for parents to pass on to daughters: 80 percent of rape victims are sixteen to twenty-four years old.

Do-nothing thinking is: "Confrontation always makes everything worse. Don't react—it might be an overreaction. When everything else is out of control, it's important to stay calm. Don't add to the violence by becoming violent yourself. Don't make him mad. Trying to escape risks escalating the problem." These ideas are wishful thinking or blind optimism. Experience at real crime scenes teaches you something different.

The do-nothing group correctly recognizes the risk in doing something, but fails to see that there is just as much risk in doing nothing. If you face a rapist and do nothing, he'll rape you. If you face an armed criminal forcing you into his car and do nothing, he'll kidnap you. Fundamentally, the do-nothing group wants protection against crime as much as the rest of us; the fallacy in their thinking is they believe that in doing nothing, they risk nothing. Instead they rely on the criminal's sudden conversion to compassion. I call this the "hope-and-luck defense." *Hope it doesn't happen to me! If I'm lucky, I won't be hurt!*

Doers, in contrast, have simple and direct reasons for taking action: *If I don't do something fast, it's going to get worse.*

An inmate in his sixties serving life in Folsom Prison for the murder of his wife and her lover speaking about young gang member criminals:

The new breed of criminals, they're really something. They'll kill you over nothing. They don't hardly ever have any reason. We used to kill guys when I was young and outside, but we had a reason. I mean, it was something like someone messing with your wife or a fight over something with another guy or maybe sometimes an armed robbery that the guy wanted to fight us and wouldn't give us the money. But there was always a reason we had, we never killed a guy just for the sake of killing him. These guys kill you in a second just as well as they look at you. I don't like being in here with them, they're too dangerous.

WHAT DOES WORK

What works, as proved by the results of police survival training, is *mind-setting.* Mind-setting is rehearsing and visualizing actions in your mind, a method used in many fields, from sports to law enforcement, military to medicine.

It's a way of planning our responses. We do something similar every day in our regular lives. We plan what to say if the boss criticizes a report we've submitted or how to appease our spouse if we've done something irritating. Often we actually rehearse the words we'll use, we do it constantly. It doesn't always get us what we want, but it gives us a better chance.

All this mental preparation is motivated by fear, minor pricks of fear that your family or colleagues will be annoyed with you. Yet most people do not mind-set against their biggest, most intense fear: injury and life-threatening violence to themselves or their family. They don't because the subject is too frightening and because they don't know how to mentally rehearse crime protection. In fact, protection against crime is simple because criminals tend to do the same thing over and over to victim after victim. Cops call that criminal habit their MO (modus operandi).

Mind-setting to survive violent crime draws on real-life crime cases, which allows us to analyze the mistakes of others, learn from them, and decide how we will respond differently. Thus, from your memory, decisions will flash back to you during an actual crisis. That gives you survival rules to fall back on in case the security of your world explodes. In a nutshell, the purpose of mind-setting against crime is to create survival dos and don'ts using "worst-case" scenario planning.

Face-to-face with violence: Your first split-second problem is not what is he going to do, but, what are you going to do. Mind-setting against violence answers that question at the right time . . . before it happens. Pure and simple, it trains your survival instincts. In peace and quiet, you use your intellect and logic ahead of time to weigh your best options, taking into account your physical limitations, your children, and their ages. This mental exercise prompts bottom-line decision-making that provides direction during the confusion and terror of a crisis when everything else is out of control, a time when most people are frozen with fear.

In training men and women police officers (SWAT or new recruits), we had them practice as much as possible. But, most life-or-death decisive responses cannot be physically practiced. So, mental rehearsal based on survival rules was our training tool.

Do people become paranoid when blasted with the horrific stories of crime victims? No. One story at a time, they develop a survival mentality by discussing with friends and families what they would have done differently, just as cops do. Not only that, in thirty years of teaching, I've noticed an additional benefit to mind-setting against violence. You not only develop a survival mentality to increase your chances at the instant violence explodes, you also develop a new alertness to crime avoidance, noticing more quickly the opening stages of possible danger.

According to Mark Leap, captain, Los Angeles Police Department:

"During the training of new police officers, the number one priority is planning ahead—mental rehearsal. Without it, cops are easy prey, and it's no different for citizens. Citizens freeze up as do cops. Even with training it happens. But cops snap out of it—most citizens don't, because they haven't planned against the worst our streets have to offer.

—

"Before planning how to survive violence, most people need an attitude change. If you believe it won't happen to you, then you're not going to plan against it. You have to face facts, crossing this threshold first: it can happen to me, exactly like it happens to others.

"Cops play what-if games in their minds, alone and with each other. Every time they read a newspaper account of something or investigate a crime, they place themselves at that crime scene. They reenact it, mentally transferring themselves into other crime situations, and plan a response. Stories, as gruesome as they may be, are an important part of survival planning. They motivate people to plan against that same crime happening against them. Some people do that, others don't. The ones who don't are easier victims."

Dr. Spencer Johnson, coauthor of the *One Minute Manager* and author of, among other books, *Yes or No: The Guide to Better Decisions,* lays it out this way:

"Good decisions are the product of a good system, and parts of that system must include: What are the probable consequences? Am I being honest with myself? Am I letting fear stop me from making any decisions?"

Without mind-setting, people freeze up; they have no way to cut through the overwhelming fear that boxes them in during a crisis.

In order to mind-set effectively, we must first learn to deal with fear.

Part II

Dealing with Fear

BREAKING THROUGH FEAR

Do exactly as you're told and I won't hurt you!
  Don't resist and you won't get hurt!
  Quit screaming or I'll kill you!
You have a choice. You can do nothing and hope you never hear these words. Or you can prepare against the paralyzing fear induced by those threats by making decisions that will allow you to control and use your fear instead of its controlling you.

The primary, overwhelming fact of criminal violence is paralyzing fear of injury. Whether you're experienced or inexperienced against violence—a prepared police officer or unprepared citizen—when you're suddenly looking down the barrel of a gun or feel the point of a knife at your neck, you're instantly frozen by fear. Your muscles automatically contract, you're terrified. The criminal is yelling life-threatening orders, and obeying seems to be your only means of survival.

The second fact of criminal violence is its incredible speed. Only seconds are needed to abduct you into a car, force you into a nearby ravine, enter your home and gain physical and emotional control of you and your family. The criminal counts on your feeling boxed in and panic-stricken—that's why he threatens you with violence.

Everything that happens after the crime goes down is initially dependent on whether you have previously torn down the walls of fear that box you in. The reason people are boxed in is always the speed, and the fear of injury. Together both are overwhelming to anyone unprepared.

When I was an officer-survival trainer, I always began training new cops with these words:

Explosive violence requires two commitments from you to survive:

1. A mental attitude that will overcome fear of injury to take extreme risks.
2. A physical response that is immediate, direct, and explosive.

A Mother-and-Daughter Story: Cindy's Story

In 1984, Wendy, my fourteen-year-old, and I participated in a crime defense course at her school in La Jolla, California. We heard things we didn't really want to hear. We were told to expect injury. I wasn't prepared for this experience to be so mentally and physically exhausting.

Over and over I wondered if we really needed to hear the awful stories being told in the program. Why couldn't we just learn how to defend ourselves without them? I didn't really want to know what happened during kidnapping and rape. But we stayed, because I have always preferred to be informed and prepared.

My friends questioned my judgment in introducing my daughter to this world of violence and crime. They feared the stories would have a devastating and negative effect on her. Well, they did have an effect, they saved her life. She listened, she remembered the stories, and she made her decision—she would refuse to submit to any attacker. She would scream, resist, and fight to protect herself.

Five years later, in 1989, when she was at college, I got a phone call one early Saturday morning in October. My daughter, who was living a half mile off campus, called to say that a man had tried to rape her and that he had cut her some. She assured me everything was under control, and there was no need to come up to be with her. I was on an airplane in ninety minutes.

A man had snuck into her house, used a knife from her own kitchen, and tried to rape her. Her response was instantaneous, thanks to her training.

I'm so pleased I didn't weaken when I began to question whether or not we should attend that real-life course. It made all the difference in her life and mine.

Wendy's Story

October 1989. I was a twenty-year-old junior at Lewis and Clark College in Portland, Oregon. I returned to my apartment at 3 A.M., having been out with friends. About a half hour later, some kind of movement woke me up. A man was sitting on my bed, rubbing my legs. At first, I thought someone I knew was joking around. I sat up, pushed him to the floor, and shouted, "Cut it out!" He sprang back, jumped on top of me, and put a knife to my throat. With his other hand he covered my mouth, crushing my face.

My body seemed to slip away from me. It was like I was stepping out of my body and seeing this happen to me. He planned to rape me, I knew it. A paralyzing fear started to overwhelm me. I could feel my strength draining away. But, just as suddenly, something in my mind shouted, "Don't give up." I was starting to feel anger. His pants were off. His knife was pressed against my neck. I remember fighting the urge to give up. He was trying to get my legs apart. Something in me was shouting, "Stop him—fight him."

It's funny what goes through your head in a crisis. I remember from the training program, we were told it would be that way, our mind would float, that we would have to fight against that. I had to concentrate, to focus.

Then I did something I never thought I was capable of: I grabbed the knife blade. With my other hand, I struggled to gouge his eyes.

I didn't have time to hesitate. I just did it. Grabbing his knife is what stopped him from raping me. I remember thinking, "You'll have to cut off my fingers, I hate you." Anger and fear drove me. I think hating him helped me hold on to the knife . . . to have made the decision: he would have to cut off my fingers before he raped me. Something inside exploded, something I didn't know was there.

He told me, "I'll kill you." I thought, "You had better mean it, you son of a bitch, because I'm going to fight this." I struggled to free my mouth. I started screaming. I have never screamed that loud. I was screaming my housemate's name—I knew she was home sleeping in the other room. Then I heard her screaming. That made him jump up. He tried to take off, to run. Blood was everywhere; on my sheets, my pillows, my face, my nightgown.

He let go of the knife when he bolted away from me and off my bed. He was trying to get his pants on and escape. I lunged after him. I had the knife in my hand. My hands were slashed and dripping with blood, but I didn't feel a thing. I remember hearing in our training program about a woman who had grabbed her attacker's knife the instant it was out of his hand. That story had stuck in my mind. I was still screaming. I should have gone the other way and escaped, but I didn't. It was as though I was no longer in control of my body. I stabbed him right in the face with his own knife as he was trying to fix his pants. He took off leaving a trail of blood. In fact, he even dropped his wallet—that's how he was caught.

I must admit to being proud that I didn't give up. I knew I must resist the attack—I had to fight it. It was just one of my personal survival decisions I learned about. A decision I had made a long time ago and didn't have to think about when it faced me. I remember believing I would win. I was going to end it now—my way, not his way. I never questioned myself. There was no time. I listened to those rape stories. They helped me make up my mind. That night, my adrenaline exploded and the action seemed to come naturally.

Another thing that helped me—I knew I was going to be cut, I expected it, so when it happened, it didn't scare me. I was badly cut, but he didn't get what he came for.

It's been several years since it all happened, and I don't always sleep well at night. I have nightmares and some bad memories. My mind goes back to that night now and then. But, I'll tell you this . . . as bad as it was, it could have been a lot worse.

What Wendy Did Wrong

Attacking him instead of escaping was a mistake. But it's not an uncommon mistake when people are on autopilot and enraged. For example, many purse-snatch victims have chased the thief and wound up badly injured. To overcome that kind of mistake, think *escape* and only *escape* when you mind-set.

What They Did Right

Cindy and Wendy did everything else right. It's never too early to prepare your children to face danger.

Wendy decided she feared rape more than injury. That was a pivotal decision. She knew she could be injured, so she wasn't paralyzed by fear.

She had made a bottom-line decision: she would make raping her the hardest thing a man ever does against her.

For the Record

Wendy recovered from her wounds, graduated, and is now a commercial photographer. She speaks to women's groups

about personal protection and has appeared on nationally tele-
vised talk shows.

Wendy's attacker was a teacher with a prior criminal record.
He was sentenced to six years for his attack on Wendy, served
two, and is now out on parole as a registered sex offender. He
got his former teaching job back.

I recall a talk show host's referring to Wendy's response
as courageous and fearless. I said to him, "Courage is
overcoming fear, not being fearless."

Fear can paralyze and panic the strongest of us or fill the
weakest with courage beyond any degree they've ever
known—courage driven by a rage-filled determination.
Which it will be for you, if you are ever targeted for a violent
crime, depends on which you fear most: injury against
yourself in trying to escape or control by the attacker and
his crimes against you?

In 1985, I read of two women psychologists who had
studied the effects of fear on women who resisted successfully or unsuccessfully during a rape attack against them.
Their findings go beyond rape and apply to every man and
woman who face violence under any condition: "The wom-
en who resisted and escaped feared rape over injury. The
women who resisted but were overpowered feared injury
above rape." I've heard the latter echoed by many rape
victims.

Note: Moms and dads have the power to affect what their
children fear and submit to, or fight against.

Following orders from a criminal—"Stay where you are,"
"Don't move"—seems like the way to escape injury. But, in
fact, blind obedience makes it easier for him to switch from
a quick theft to violence against you. Unless you have made
decisions about what you will do ahead of time, you'll be
frozen with fear and confusion.

We have a completely different reaction to accidents or

natural disasters—a house fire, a capsized boat, or an auto accident. In facing these crises, men and women move into action with speed, decisiveness, and courage far beyond what they believed possible from themselves. Your physical resources are galvanized by fear of the consequences and fueled by a clear need to act.

But commands from criminals stop us cold. The need to act is blurred by his orders telling us *not* to act. We're scared; then our intellect begins to analyze based on incorrect assumptions: "If I do as I am told, he says he won't hurt me; makes sense to me. I won't give him any reason to injure me." We're civilized, sensible, reasonable people who base decisions on logic, and we tend to believe what we hear—especially in a crisis involving violence, we hear what we want to hear: I won't get hurt . . . if I obey him.

It is essential to remember that initial injury is far from the worst consequence of violent crime. Once he has you under control and isolated, you very likely face death, and as a woman, torture and rape, too.

If what you fear more than anything else is injury, you will not have the determination necessary to escape a criminal attack. Never. When frozen by fear of injury, you will believe all the criminal's promises, you'll be unable to concentrate on saving yourself, and you'll never notice any fleeting opportunities to escape. The criminal will use your fear to control everything you do. Then you're his— "bought and paid for," as cops refer to it.

For example, most mass murderers are single assailants who must reload their weapons. How many have died because they were paralyzed with fear and were then shot during the second or third fusillade?

In 1984, in a San Ysidro, California, fast-food-restaurant massacre, the killer had three weapons; he reloaded all three weapons twice, yet no one moved. In 1993, Colin Ferguson walked backward through the third car of the 5:33 P.M. Long Island Rail Road commuter train and shot people at random, left and right, with a 9mm semiautomatic. He killed five, wounded nineteen, and was reloading for the second time when someone yelled, "Grab him!" One passenger tackled Ferguson in the center of the car, then two more men piled onto him. It always happens at crime scenes; when one person breaks through fear, others find courage and follow him.

I call it crime-scene leadership. In October 1994, it happened again in Washington, D.C., when Francisco Duran opened fire on the White House with a semiautomatic rifle. One of several bystanders tackled him from behind. Instantly, another man ran forward and helped subdue him.

More than all our other emotions combined, fear directs our lives. Whether it be fear of something simple or great, applause or boos, life or death.

To break out of paralyzing fear at a time of violence, you must *redirect or convert your fear of injury into primitive rage against your attacker.* Never stop fearing him and what he can do to you, but rechannel the power of that emotion into hatred for him. Once you do that, your concentration is no longer blocked. You're able to seize opportunities when they arise and can perform almost superhuman feats. You've heard of parents who saved their children from burning buildings collapsing around them or lifted cars off a family member pinned underneath. When not blocked by a controlling fear of injury, human beings draw on incredible strength in moments of crisis.

To survive criminal violence, you need to muster and concentrate every resource available to you for a few desperate seconds. Those resources are all the powers of your mind and body directed by the emotional force of your fear. Combine that with anger, and you'll have two emotions that will drive you to extraordinary, undreamt-of animal strength in times of danger. It's known as our fight-or-flight response. These are the resources that give us the ability to put our lives on the line. It doesn't take extraordinary people, it takes ordinary people faced with extraordinary circumstances.

The Bottom Line

Break through paralyzing fear with two steps:

1. Decide what you fear most: being injured or being controlled by a criminal. Accepting injury as the price we pay to escape violence is crucial.
2. Mind-set against your fears by visualizing how you will escape. That focuses you on escaping him instead of obeying him.

FIGHT-OR-FLIGHT RESPONSE

When your life is threatened, your emotions race and your body prepares for confrontation. It takes place in fractions of a second and in the same way to man and animal. Blood pressure rises and extra adrenaline is pumped into the bloodstream. Breathing and heart rates speed up, your lungs work faster and longer. Everything in you is getting ready to do what is necessary to survive. You don't control these changes, they happen to all of us. It's called our fight-or-flight response.

If it's dark, our eyes dilate and immediately we see better. Our digestive system shuts down, diverting blood into our muscles. Suddenly we're stronger. Our blood even thickens to slow bleeding from wounds. Endorphins are released, and instantly we feel less pain and thus are less distracted and concentrate better. Sugar and carbohydrate reserves are released, making explosive energy available. Physically, we are unstoppable.

Our visual perception alters so that we see everything in slow motion (this is called tachypsychia), which also allows us to concentrate better and use the extraordinary energy our body has made available. This slow-motion phenomenon always accompanies life-or-death resistance and severe injury. I have heard it reported by victim after victim, cops and citizens, and I've experienced it personally.

The more stressful the circumstances, the closer we come to achieving our maximum potential. The entire fight-or-flight changes in your body have one purpose: to give you more power and better concentration on survival during a life-threatening crisis.

In primitive times, this response was necessary to survive constant physical danger. Today, while it is still necessary for surviving violence, we have become accustomed to shutting down our fight-or-flight response—we call this being civilized. Society cannot function if we go around exploding whenever we don't get our way when someone steals our parking space or the soccer coach yells at our child. We are conditioned by society to keep this powerful force in check, to look for alternatives to releasing our explosive fight-or-flight power. That self-restraint works well for us as long as we're dealing with other civilized human beings. It dooms us when we're up against a criminal.

A criminal's commands and threats of death short-circuit this natural resource by activating our fear of injury. The result is that in times of criminal violence, too many people end up being cut off from the very resource they most need. The solution is to retrain your instincts through mind-setting to instantly switch from your civilized intellectual response to your primitive fight-or-flight response.

EXPECT TO BE INJURED

To survive criminal violence, you must first overcome your paralyzing fear of injury. Not only are we terrified by physical threat, the civilized mind has been trained since infancy to be reasonable, to negotiate instead of using force. We have also been conditioned to believe that other people are reasonable, sensible beings. So when we are confronted with violence and hear words like "Do what I say and you won't get hurt," we're in complete shock, petrified of being hurt, and then we leap to believe the false promises that offer us safety.

We all necessarily fall back on our own limited experience. Or as the journalist Walter Lippman put it, "We too often believe that the world we experience is the sum total of the world that exists."

Much of my "How to Survive" teaching efforts are aimed at getting others to accept what they don't want to accept. Part of that "acceptance" is, few civilized people have any past experiences to relate to when thrust into a time of violence. For most people, their worst experience was a screaming, shouting (maybe shoving and slugging) match involving family or friends. No comparison to a violent crime.

Violent criminals are like nothing the average person has ever experienced. They are psychopaths, which means they release their anger and they get their kicks from senselessly hurting or killing other people. Many of them don't care whether they live or die. They may sound and look like anyone else, they are often friendly, but that's only so they can get what they want—control over others, then the injuries begin.

You can't imagine threatening to kill another human being if he doesn't get into the trunk of your car, or to blow off the head of a three-year-old. We can't imagine ourselves thinking it, let alone voicing it. They do both. In being or becoming a violent person, thinking about violence is the first step. The second is talking about it. The third step is doing it. Cops have seen those one-two-three steps enough to accept them as reality.

Acknowledging this difference between yourself and

violence-addicted criminals will spur you to develop a reality-based point of reference. The first move toward your new point of reference is to go over the stories of those who have had firsthand experience with violent crime.

People with experience against violent crime know they must expect injury. It's a lousy expectation. But if criminal violence strikes, you have only lousy choices. It's an acceptance of reality:

- Do something: try to escape, take the risk now, accept the injury, or
- Do nothing: obey, do everything he says, and take the risk later.

You'll have split seconds to decide. Never forget, violent criminals have rap sheets . . . all of them: they're recidivists. They also have two choices:

- Allow you to live, or
- Leave no witnesses.

No amount of pleading or reason or promises will help you. He will do to you whatever he has done to others like you in the past. If you believe him, you'll obey him—that's what he needs to easily control you. If you let your fear of injury control you, you're doomed. Because then you'll suppress, you'll shut down your incredible fight-or-flight power. Then, a criminal easily makes every decision affecting your life or death.

HARD-LINE APPROACH

People who don't want to hear about risk or injury want a soft-line approach to surviving violent crime. The worst-case scenarios, used in hard-line training, are abhorrent to them. Soft-line training protects people from hearing about the truly frightening aspects of real crime. Some teachers of limited experience are wrong when they say things like, "If you're under attack, take a deep breath to calm yourself and help you focus before acting." Any cop with a career of experience at major crime scenes will say flat out you don't have take-a-deep-breath time when someone is choking you or thrusting a gun between your eyes. It's a calming thought to hear, but it doesn't play out at a crime scene involving violence.

When everything in your world crumbles and you're facing death, hard-line survival training and tough-minded decisions are the only preparation that can pull you through against the worst of criminals. You need something that works against the worst because you get no second chances.

Steve McIntire joined the San Diego Police Department in 1978 and was in our training program. He was skeptical about the value of hard-line training, until he faced two killers.

Steve McIntire's Story

August 1980. I was twenty-three, a hard charger. On the graveyard shift, a routine fight call came in from the heart of the Crips and Bloods gang territory, and I was the first on the scene in a one-man squad car. The fight was over, everyone had scattered. I positioned my car so I could see well and began writing in my journal. Two guys came out of the Crip house and walked in my direction. I didn't feel any fear at that moment. Frankly, I had become complacent, working that area for so long. Suddenly, one of the Crips was knocking on my right window to distract me. Suddenly, on my left my worst nightmare was going down. I felt the steel of a gun on the back of my neck. I remember my body racing to protect my head, but my mind was questioning everything my gut was telling me—almost like I was telling myself, "This isn't really happening."

I couldn't get my own gun out because it was jammed up against the door—I'm left-handed—which was probably a blessing because I didn't waste the one second I had trying to fast-draw. I went into autopilot. My mind raced back to what we were taught in the academy. Our instructors said, "You will fall back on this training." They used to shout at us, "When at point-blank range, hemmed in, pinned down, the gun is on you and being fired, go for the gun . . . get the barrel off you— concentrate on the barrel. Concentrate."

Thank God, my instincts and training took over. Our defensive-tactics instructors were always so insistent, so serious. Especially Strong. I didn't like his hard-and-fast rules. Frankly, I thought he was a hard-line asshole. But I figured these guys had been around the block, so I listened and that's what saved my life.

I turned and got both hands on the gun. It was only a split second, but suddenly I saw the frantic, panicked look in the Crip's face. It wasn't going the way he had planned. At that same instant, the gun went off. The lights seemed blinding. My mouth felt like I had taken a blow from a baseball bat at full swing. The feeling was odd and in slow motion. I don't know where I got the power, but I held on to the gun and physically pulled the guy into the car. He let go of the gun and ran. The last thing I saw was both of them running down the street.

I slumped over the steering wheel, blood gushing out of my mouth. "I've been shot, I'm gonna die," I remember thinking. "I'm too young to die . . . I've got too much in front of me. I'm not through yet." I screamed into the radio, "Emergency! Eleven ninety-nine!" When I did that, blood really poured.

I could hear sirens everywhere. What a great sound! My buddies were coming. I saw the first car speed by. "God, he can't see me!" I realized. I opened my mouth, blood gushed again, but I still yelled into the night. It was Bill; he heard me, did a 180-degree turn on all four wheels, and skidded right up to me. He got me into his car and took off.

I've had lots of time to think about what pulls people through the worst crisis in their lives. It's training—and it better be training before the hammer falls. That Crip taught me that the hard-line style of survival training made the difference. They told us, "You're going to get hurt." And it was that way for me that night. I couldn't stop them from shooting me, but I stopped them from killing me.

What Steve Did Wrong

Steve momentarily let his guard down. Cops and citizens alike are less alert and more vulnerable when comfortably habituated to a routine and an environment.

What He Did Right

When the attack went down, Steve fell back on training. He put it this way: "Anyone who ever faces a real criminal better have some 'face-reality' training up front. That Crip taught me that night that soft, easygoing training would never have held up against him. Being a cop didn't make the difference. It never does when it's life or death. It's hard-line survival training that makes the difference."

For the Record

Steve's injuries have healed, but they forced him to leave law enforcement. The two gang members are in prison.

Remember, our minds tend to "float" some when facing death—to other times less serious and to our loved ones.

Every man and woman who has faced death, suffered serious injury, and survived will relate the same phenomenon to you. The solution: force concentration upon yourself . . . you'll then feel an aimed power building within you.

Part III

Mind-Setting Against Violence

The fundamental principle of surviving violence is mental. Not physical, not gadgetry, but mental preparation, mind-setting. It consists of visualizing a crime scene and mentally rehearsing your response. Mind-setting gives you this crucial advantage when violence strikes: "This is not new to me, I've thought about this before. I know what to do." Then your instincts trained for this moment will kick in.

There are three steps. They work because they're simple, and steps one and two are familiar to you in other aspects of your life.

1. Visualize yourself in the crime scene . . . *not near it, in it.*
2. Visualize your actions toward escape . . . *see yourself as explosive as you've ever been.*
3. Visualize being shot or stabbed . . . *not easy to do but crucial.*

These three steps have one objective. Escape violence — not stand and fight.

The first important issue is to use real-life crime cases. You won't get much information from reading a newspaper or watching the news on television, but even out at the scene you'll only have bits of information and gut feelings. You don't need minute-by-minute details to mind-set your escape-and-survive response. Too much detail is counter-productive. Keep it quick and clean.

Step one: Picturing yourself at the scene forces you to respond, which in turn forces you to make risk-filled decisions based on what's best for your survival, not on the attacker's threats.

Step two: Visualizing your actions toward escape provides you with your own orders to follow instead of his. Your mind will be clogged: "Is this really happening?" You'll be fumbling with strategies and tactics and not knowing what to do first. Having one objective, which you have chosen ahead of time, helps you to concentrate during a crisis.

Step three: The crucial and the most overlooked juncture is expecting to get hurt. "Expect to be injured," maybe seriously, is a gaping hole in too many crime-protection plans. It is crucially important because a person who is not prepared to be injured is not fully prepared against violent crime. Most people, including police officers, have never been seriously injured, let alone shot or knifed. Without the expectation of injury, injury freezes everyone up. Visualize yourself being shot or stabbed ahead of time and you minimize the chance you'll freeze up if it happens. People say, "I was overwhelmed with the fear of dying"; "It just overwhelmed me and stopped me." Freezing up is nothing more than your fear being in control rather than you being in control.

I don't claim to have invented visualization or mind-setting. I took a proven mental-conditioning process and made it applicable to surviving violence.

Mind-setting affords a practical means of rehearsing against life-threatening violence in an uncomplicated, quick, privacy-of-your-mind way. It's based on immediate reaction—not on weapons and gadgets. After learning of a crime case that could have hit you, take a few minutes alone or with a family member to make personal survival decisions. Keep it simple and direct, uncomplicated. Don't keep mulling over details. The strength of mind-setting is having straightforward decisions to fall back on when under the pressure of a life-or-death crisis. You must see yourself rage-filled, yelling, running, exactly as you would if your child's life were at stake. Mind-setting to survive violence with these three steps is the vehicle cops and citizens use to develop a survival mentality.

The subconscious mind controls most of our first reactions during all types of crises. Contrary to popular misconceptions, the subconscious is far from irrational. Rather, our learned experiences, real or imagined, are stored there, waiting to direct and control our movements in dire circumstances and under the extreme pressure of life-threatening situations. And our subconscious is one-track—that's why so many people "freeze up" in the face of a life-or-death emergency. They have little to no experience with such a situation, and if they have not imagined what to do, they have no starting point—they're immobilized with fear. Conversely, men and women with survival decisions made move into an immediate response because their "subconscious" directs them.

The conscious, decision-making, or option-choosing part of our mind is multitrack. It takes in a lot of different information simultaneously and processes it. The processing takes time, but we do this normally as part of our regular, daily lives. Under violent assault, you have only split seconds and an overload of confusing, threatening information coming in at you. Your muscles and mind lock up. That's when your subconscious mind, *if it is prepared with simple directives,* takes over and snaps you out of paralysis in the crucial first seconds of any crisis.

Crime stories give you the vicarious experience to role-play with yourself as the central character. At the crucial time you will remember stories of attacks against others. I know it personally and I have heard this repeatedly from fellow officers and crime victims. I still remember the stories that flashed through my mind when I was attacked as a police officer—the stories that helped me pull through.

Kathleen Sullivan, whose story is ahead, was attacked by a rapist. She says, "When he put that knife to my throat, I knew he was not just trying to rape me, he was going to cut me up, too, like the stories I'd heard. I knew I had nothing to lose!"

Wendy, whose story you've already read, said, "When he put his hand on my mouth, his knife at my throat, I was terrified. Instantly, I recalled a woman talking about how she was raped and how it changed her life. When I heard her describe what she went through, I made a decision . . . that any man who tries to rape me will be faced with the hardest thing he has ever done. That decision made the difference for me. At that moment, I began to fight."

There's another advantage from mind-setting against crime besides increased alertness to crime avoidance. If crime strikes you, it will most likely strike in a place familiar to you where you have already imagined it might happen. This is because when you visualize a crime happening, you will not picture the real victim, you will picture yourself. You will not picture it happening in their home or office, but

This was my first experience in how mind-setting works:

In 1966, I was at the San Diego police academy and our trainer was Sgt. A. D. Brown. One day he mentioned casually, "By the way, if your car is ever firebombed, hit the gas. Get the hell out of there. Don't bolt from your car. Stay in it. High speed will put the fire out."

Whoa! Wait a minute! Too risky! Cars on fire blow up. I used to watch too much television, and blowing up is what cars always do on television. (In my twenty years on the force, and all the car fires I've seen, I've never seen one blow up.) So I asked, "Why not bolt from the car?"

Sergeant Brown, always blunt, answered, "Young man, if your car is on fire, you have three choices and one second to decide. Your first choice is to sit in your car and do nothing and see if you burn up, too. [I rejected that one right away.] Your second choice is to open the door fast, jump out, and try to beat the fire as it instantly engulfs the inside of your car and sears your lungs, because the oxygen sucks it in. [Damn, I didn't like the sound of that one either.] Your third choice is, do as I say. Hit the gas."

I learned two important lessons that day: what to do if my car is firebombed, and that sometimes big problems have simple solutions — like hit the gas!

Two years later, my partner and I were in our car and a part of a force at a store-burning riot scene. A firebomb hit about five or ten feet away. Not a direct hit, but close enough to cover the right side and the front and rear of the car in flames. I was one scared cop. Before I realized what I was doing, I had hit the gas. A. D. Brown's advice had come back and taken over. I was on autopilot. Within seconds, the only danger I was facing was high speed. My partner was yelling, "Slow down! Slow down!" A few blocks, the fire was out. I was shocked. Brown was right, it worked.

in yours. You will visualize your car, the mall parking lot you frequent, the streets you normally drive. Visualizing the places you frequent, a natural phenomenon, helps you this way: 80 percent of all crime occurs in the three places where you spend most of your time—your home or adjacent to it, your place of work and its parking lot, and the public routes you travel regularly, including where you jog, walk, Rollerblade. For students, the locale includes their campus. This 80 percent fact actually dictates the training and safeguarding of high-profile, likely-target VIPs.

When you and your family make bottom-line survival decisions or do mind-setting, you get no guarantee that none of you will ever be hurt by crime. What you do get is your best chance; you even the odds because of planning. When the criminal plans his crime, he's more difficult to escape. When you plan your escape, you're no longer his easy, next victim. You're a lot of trouble. And for many criminals, you just may not be worth the risk.

YOUR NEW SURVIVAL MIND-SET

Here's how to use a real-life crime case to mind-set:

Prisoner kills driver during escape here

Sheriff's deputy is seriously hurt in futile pursuit

BY FRANK KLIMKO
AND L. ERIK BRATT
Staff Writers

A jail inmate being taken to a downtown San Diego correctional facility last night escaped from a Sheriff's Department van and bludgeoned a female sheriff's deputy before seizing a car and killing the driver.

—

The inmate, identified by sheriff's authorities as 34-year-old Jonathan George, was still at large late last night. He was described as black, 6 feet tall, 240 pounds, with a mustache, and wearing a green jump suit.

George was being held to answer state criminal charges. He was being taken with another inmate from an El Cajon jail facility when he escaped about 9 p.m., according to Sheriff Jim Roache. The van was in the Gaslamp Quarter when Georged kicked open a window and took off, said Roache, who arrived at the scene just after the incident.

The sheriff's deputy, a 58-year-old woman, chased George for about two blocks before tackling him on the street, Roache said. George beat the deputy senseless and took her gun, and then confronted a taxi driver, who refused to give up his car, officers said.

George then proceeded to the intersection of Fifth Avenue and G Street, where he confronted the driver of a 1989 Honda Civic who was stopped at a red light, authorities said.

George brandished the deputy's gun and ordered the driver to get out of the car. When the driver refused, George shot him and dumped his body onto the pavement, witnesses said.

"The car never stopped moving, man," another witness said. "He just yanked the body out and threw it down on the pavement."

A passenger in the car was able to escape unharmed.

The area where the shooting occurred is a popular nightspot for downtown theatergoers, and the shooting happened at the height of the dinner hour, almost directly in front of the restaurant Trattoria La Strada.

The names of the injured sheriff's deputy and the dead driver were not immediately available. The law officer was hospitalized.

Carjacking, which involves stealing a car while the owner is still in it, is a growing trend. Police have said 165 vehicles have been taken from their owners this year in San Diego, and the numbers appear to be increasing.

Guns have been the most commonly used weapon, followed by knives and clubs. Until now, victimized drivers have suffered only minor injuries, police say.

Let's look at two different responses to this story. When the husband comes home, the average family discussion goes something like this:

SHE: Honey, did you read about that man murdered right downtown close to your office?

HE: Yeah. Poor guy. He didn't have a chance. Nothing he could do.

SHE: He was just executed in his own car.

HE: There's no place safe anymore. It's real upsetting.

Focusing on the senselessness, the tragedy, the inability to affect the outcome, is a natural reaction to such a story. However, you learn nothing. By visualizing yourself in this crisis, you can turn this into a learning opportunity like this:

SHE: Honey, did you read about that man murdered right downtown close to your office?

HE: Yeah. I was thinking about it on the way home.

SHE: We've been on that same street at that same hour several times.

HE: I know. I would like to talk about it, in case that happens to us. We'll both start by yelling, "Get out, gun! Get out, gun!" and we bolt and run.

SHE: What if the kids are with us?

HE: Let's talk about that next. First, let's get ourselves in sync.

Note: What to do when your children are with you is explained in detail in the "Carjacking" section.

SHE: Okay. And no arguing with him or grabbing my purse or your briefcase.

HE: Right.

SHE: Why not hit the gas like the cabdriver did?

HE: Great! You're right. He tried to get a cabbie's car before he killed that man, but the cabbie hit the gas instantly.

SHE: The paper said that probably saved his life.

HE: Okay. Let's make this decision: if we have the space in front of us—no traffic and our car is running—we'll hit the gas. But if we can't do that in a split second, we bolt from the car.

Note: The next part of a conversation like this one is, "What if he shoots at us or actually shoots one of us?" That subject and your family decision require more explanation from me—you'll read that in Rule #1.

For the Record

Jonathon George was a rapist, armed robber, home intruder, twice-imprisoned, twice-released career criminal. In October 1992, he was arrested again for seven more serious crimes and was being transferred from one jail to another. He overpowered a deputy sheriff, armed himself with her gun, and was looking for a getaway car.

• First attempt — a woman had just parked her minivan and was locking the doors and warding off a panhandler-would-be-window-washer when George shoved the gun into her face and flung her fifteen feet. Terrified, injured, and screaming, she got to her feet and took off, never looking back. The minivan keys were lost during the melee.

• Second attempt— within seconds, George hit a cabdriver,

shoving the gun into his face. The cabbie responded instantly by hitting the gas and was gone.

• Third attempt — George turned to the next approaching car. Desperate and ready to kill, he shoved the gun into the driver's face. Reacting in a natural way, the driver said, "Hey — get outta here!" George instantly murdered him and flung his body from the car, as the passenger bolted and ran. George took off with the car.

In media stories, you would not be aware of the details I've just given you, nor is that information crucial to your survival decision. News stories in the paper and on television give an overview. That's all you need to mind-set. Remember, a survival mentality works best when your response is immediate, direct, and explosive — no exceptions. Too many details will clog up everything, complicate your planning, and slow your response.

Mark D. Ferrell, former U.S. Secret Service agent:

For Secret Service agents, charged with protection of people, mind-setting, going over and over worst-case scenarios in your mind, is a major part of preparation. In fact, part of the exam for the job was based on an applicant's ability to mentally make life-or-death decisions from just one photograph. Agents are shown videotapes of past assassinations and attempted assassinations of both U.S. and other world leaders. Not so different nor much more than you see on the news. We used that TV footage as training aides in what should and shouldn't be done. One example: When Ford was president, two people tried to kill him. Once was when he was exiting a hotel. She began shooting from across the street at him. The agents pushed President Ford down, alongside the armored limousine. While watching the news footage, every once in a while you'd see his head coming up, looking to see what was going on, along with the agents. From that footage we altered some decisions in how to save the life of the president. Like: The door should be already open, because there's no better spot to be in but in the armored limo, instead of alongside it. When President Reagan was shot, at the hotel in Washington, D.C., the door of his limo was open. That decision and the agent's quickness saved the president's life. What this type of training — mental conditioning— does is to open your eyes more clearly to "what's going on around me" and then provides for a quicker reaction to future deadly situations. Then, when situations occur in real life, you flip into action, you were there, you know how to do it, you've done it before.

I can remember so many, many long hours of standing in a hotel hallway, in front of the president's doorway or standing in a fire escape, or a street, waiting for him to arrive, and running through your mind, "What do I do if . . .?" Secret Service agents learned four primary things to do during an explosive and dangerous situation: (1) Sound off, so other people near you know you're in danger. (2) Cover the protectee. (3) Evacuate, get the hell out of there. (4) "Arm's reach"— if you're close, take out the assailant.

Obviously, these primary action rules apply to a Secret Service agent protecting a dignitary . . . and not to a family. The important concept is to have rules to move into action with, whatever your lifestyle.

Mind-set against one type of crisis and the decisions will lead you through other similar crises . . . always.

As a young cop riding around in a patrol car, I concentrated my mind-setting against sniper fire and being ambushed (in the late sixties, riots, snipers, and cops being ambushed were big-time). My partner and I had our car windows smashed countless times, but we were never hit by a sniper. Instead, it was a firebomb that put that particular mind-setting into action.

Susan Karsh (her story is in "The Escape-and-Survive Family Drill") went through mind-setting against an intruder with her two young girls. But, it was a fire that destroyed her home. She said, "We responded identically the way we had planned in case of an intruder."

Mind-setting to survive today's random violence is crucial in your hometown or away on vacation and business trips because this means of crime survival doesn't depend on devices and weapons that must be carried, it doesn't depend on avoiding all areas that "might" be dangerous. Nor does your safety heavily depend on the up-and-down crime trends of places you live, work, or visit. Instead, it (mind-setting) replaces much of that with the ability to switch instantly from a relaxed state of mind to a survival state of mind. Without confusion, you fall back on trained instincts.

YOUR NEW ATTITUDE

One day at a time, one crime scene after another, young law enforcement officers learn quickly that their first line of defense is their newly trained survival instincts. That training begins with their attitude toward people and situations. When cops meet people unknown to them, on duty or off, they tend to be quick to size them up, make decisions based on little hard information, a hunch. Some say they're cynical, too quick to believe the worst, too reactionary. But, the facts are, it's listening to your gut-level instinct, not your intellect.

Many citizens reverse that "gut-instinct first, intellect second" and wait to react until it's too late and beyond their control. The two primary reasons behind their hesitation are fear of looking stupid by overreacting and fear of hurting someone's feelings. Violence in America should push all citizens to the cop's attitude of "my safety first, your feelings second."

Your new attitude should include an awareness of where you are and what's going on around you. It's like when you're driving: you check the rearview mirror, watch for flashing brake lights up ahead, quickly rehearse the turns you'll be making . . . all at once.

Always consider the circumstances. Are you alone on a sparsely traveled street or in an empty parking lot? Are you about to enter an unattended vestibule or bank lobby while being followed by someone you think suspicious? Being approached by a panhandler at three in the afternoon on Central Park West should produce a different response in your gut than when you're approached by that same panhandler in the same place at midnight.

When I'm approached on the street by someone who activates a bad feeling in me, I look him in the eye, acknowledge him, nod no, and for a few steps, I keep him in my peripheral vision.

I'm not suggesting that you adopt all the attitudes of cops, just their survival attitude. Law enforcement officers are not insensitive nor hardened, except when the issue is safety. Then their attitude is fixed. They won't compromise. They've seen the results of those who did.

Jonathan Oberman, New York City public defender:

In my experience, if you want to stay alive, it's better to offend others than to act on liberal impulses. I regret when I've hurt others' feelings. I'm angered to live in a society that causes such a necessity, but I live with those feelings because I don't want to be a statistic.

Paul Pfingst, San Diego County district attorney and a former prosecuting attorney in Miami, New York City, and San Diego, describes one of his worst cases.

Manhattan Vestibule

A young New York nurse, in her thirties, living with her mother, returned to her apartment building at dusk. She entered the vestibule of the building and checked her mailbox.

Two men, one on parole for murder, loitering in the area followed her into the vestibule. One carried a hand-sized rock, probably picked up outside the building. We don't know what was said to her in the initial seconds while inside the vestibule, but it was probably something to put her at ease with their presence. One grabbed her and the other smashed the rock into her skull. They stuffed a rag into her mouth and used her keys to unlock the door leading into the main lobby. Half-walking, half-dragging her, they took her up three stories to the rooftop where they raped and sodomized her. Then they began protracted sexual torture. They cut and sliced her torso and genitals. In the end, she suffocated on her own vomit because the rag was stuffed so tightly into her mouth.

Her best chance was to lock the door behind her or walk right back out: inconvenient, maybe she would have offended someone, but safer.

My safety first, your feelings second.

DEADLY MISTAKES

From a cop's point of view, citizens seem to keep making the same mistakes over and over, until all cases begin to sound alike. What follows are some of the most common mistakes.

Instead of escaping, men try to overpower the attacker. That's the reason more men are killed at crime scenes than women. Forget the traditional revenge attitude of "Catch 'em, hold 'em, make 'em pay." The odds are against you. When it comes to priorities at crime scenes, women are way ahead of men—they focus on escape.

The "catch 'em, hold 'em, make 'em pay" reflex we men have leaves many of our families fatherless. If you and your loved ones are safe, the crook is not worth going after and he's damn sure not worth dying for. Some of the most lump-in-your-throat places I've been are private homes with husband and fathers lying dead in a woman's arms after giving his life to catch a dirtbag breaking into his parked car.

Forget about disarming the criminal. There are no sure or safe ways to disarm an attacker. If you're not a cop, obligated to arrest armed attackers, don't try it. *Your* duty is to *escape.* Reduce the danger, don't increase it.

The two most common mistakes made at crime scenes:

• Believing the criminal—the most repeated mistake and the worst because it cedes control to the criminal and sets the stage for yet more mistakes. Don't believe a word . . . violent criminals begin as emotionally disturbed children, and it's when they're young that they learn to lie. It becomes a part of their young and tortured life. One of the problems for us is by the time that child is a young adult criminal, they have perfected lying.

• Waiting for the best moment to make a move—once a crime goes down, the safe time has already passed; your real concern should be what is certain to happen if you do nothing. You can't count on a perfect opportunity.

The objective of the violent criminal is to control you, emotionally and physically. Everything he does—his threats and promises—is intended to terrify and control you. The more control you give to the violent criminal, even if you see it as temporary, the less likely you are to escape. For most crime victims, their temporary cooperation backfired into full control over them. Time works against the victim and for the criminal. The longer you stall, the more you talk, the deeper you sink.

The Four Survival Rules to Live By

It's your decision: accept victimization and whatever follows it as beyond your ability to stop, or demand of yourself escape and survival. Whichever, it's a mind-set you alone set, you alone prepare yourself with. The drive to survive must come from you.

The key elements that most benefit a violent criminal are time, isolation, and control.

The Four Rules work directly against all three. In moments of explosive violence, you face extreme danger and must take extreme risks with a physical response that is immediate, direct, and explosive. That's what mind-setting with these rules helps you do: it gives you the ability to make a crucial mental switch from everyday routine behavior to responding to life-or-death emergency.

These rules, culled from years of accumulated police experience with violence, can help save your life. They interconnect, one leads directly into the other. If you have made these rules the cornerstone of your mind-setting to survive and escape violence, they will sound in your brain and help trigger an immediate reaction toward escape—it will seem as though you're on autopilot.

The Four Rules are:

- *React immediately*—your best chance to escape violence and minimize injury is in the first seconds.
- *Resist*—your only alternative is to submit; both choices are lousy, but resisting gives you the best chance.
- *Crime scene #2*—always more isolated than the initial point of contact, and always worse for you.
- *Never, never give up*—your attitude can keep you alive when you're badly injured.

When you read or hear crime stories, rehearse how you would apply these key rules at the crucial moments. The stories here are told by the victims because they alone know what was in their minds during the attack. They know what pulled them through the most terrifying moments of their lives and made it possible for them to escape, and to survive. You will notice a certain repetition in the stories because criminals all tend to do the same things (they develop a winning routine based on controlling the victim through fear), and as I've said, men and women tend to make the same mistakes, over and over. When victims describe what they did right, they often use the same words: "I was on autopilot," "I don't know how I did it, I just did it." The repetition will help the stories stay with you.

Real courage and extraordinary action don't always come from highly trained, well-armed, and physically conditioned professionals. More often, they come from ordinary people faced with extraordinary situations who face the fact that *it's up to me to get myself out of this*.

RULE #1: REACT IMMEDIATELY

An armed stranger jumps you. These first few seconds are as good as it's going to get. With each second that passes, the more opportunity he has to hurt or kill you. Time always works against the victim. Expect the worst—statistics show that he's almost certainly a career criminal.

Armed Assault

An off-duty cop friend of mine was accosted by an armed assailant. Before the criminal even said a word, my friend shouted, *"It's all yours, take it, I'm outta here!"*

Do the same. Don't wait to find out what the attacker wants. Make an assumption and act: "Here's my wallet. Here are my car keys." Give up everything you've got immediately. Yes, it will be a hassle to replace everything. Yes, the criminal will know your address. (One high-profile businessman I know won't carry pictures of his family in his wallet.) Remember, the problems you face later can be dealt with—you've got to survive the crisis you're facing now first.

Don't get tricky throwing your belongings in opposite directions. Make it easy for him. One thing I try to avoid doing is making an armed attacker mad.

Throw him your car keys and tell him they're for the blue Mercedes over there. It doesn't matter if the blue Mercedes isn't yours, lie to him.

Then run, escape. Run anywhere. Don't complicate your situation by asking yourself "Where?" or "What direction?" At this point, anywhere you go will be an improvement. Run fast, don't zigzag or stoop low, forget the television antics.

You have a choice here. You can instantly give up your property and run, or you can be forced to give up your property and see what happens next. In other words, risk it now or risk it later. Whatever you do, you can't escape the risk.

Be the most willing and compliant robbery victim that robber has all week. If he's just a robber, great, it's over. If he's more than a robber, trying to escape is still your best chance to prevent the robbery from becoming a kidnapping, rape, or worse.

Nothing generates more interest during training than my saying, "Give up the property and get going." Taking action that contradicts the orders of an armed attacker ("One move and you're dead!") seems recklessly foolhardy. But your only other option is to do nothing at all and leave yourself at his mercy. Remember this statistic: 10 percent of all completed robberies with a compliant victim end in murder anyway. (In comparison, less than 1 percent of rape victims are killed.)

Also remember, the nature of a criminal is to lie: "Do as you're told and I won't hurt you" only carries weight in your mind—not his. Career criminals are not promise-keepers.

If he's just a robber, he wants to get your money and get out fast. An armed robber who is only after property doesn't hang around. The last thing he wants is to increase the odds of someone else happening along and people getting a good look at him. If you hand over your property and run, he will, too—*if* he's just a robber. And, if he's not, you don't want to be hanging around to find out.

The problem is we can't tell if the assailant is just a robber, or if he's also a rapist and/or killer. If he's a killer, he will likely do one of two things: execute you on the spot and take your property, or move you, then execute you and take your property. If he's also a rapist, he will usually move the woman before raping her. Of the rape victims in America who are also murdered, all are cornered in an isolated spot, such as a home or apartment, or moved to an isolated spot, then raped and murdered.

People often ask, "If I'm attacked, how will I know he's armed?" He will show you because he wants you to know. That's the point of being armed — to control you through fear. During the late sixties, a group of revolutionists in America distributed an underground publication on how to commit a crime effectively. They advised:

• Keep the weapon in view.
• Push it close in and point it at the head.
• Hit them in the head with the weapon.

The principles that work effectively to terrorize and control people don't change, so we must.

Don't wait to be told, "Turn around. Kneel. Get in the trunk." React immediately. Bolt and run. You'll never know what you missed.

Bob Ring, a thirty-five-year veteran of law enforcement in San Diego, specialized in murder, the most serious of rape cases, kidnapping, and serious crimes against children. He describes one of his successful cases.

Kidnapped Child

A twelve-year-old girl was kidnapped near a shopping center and driven to the mountains, where the kidnapper forced her into the brush. She was fighting and resisting all the way, gutsy little girl. He finally choked her unconscious. She was out for a few seconds. During that time, he ripped part of her clothing off, and when she came to, she saw him holding a knife next to her vagina. She exploded. She rolled away from him and broke into a clearing and took off running. He chased her and stabbed her deep in her right shoulder. She didn't even break stride. He was chasing her with an upraised knife. Three shooters target-practicing up on a hill some distance away saw this. They started shooting at the guy. The little girl got away. So did the attacker. I wish they had been better marksmen.

Later, when she was out of the hospital, she and I started visiting parking lots. She finally identified the car, a Singer. I had never heard of a Singer. I put it out on the radio, and within thirty minutes we had the guy.

Capturing him meant a lot to me because it also meant we solved another case involving a nine-year-old girl. He had taken that little girl to the same place, molested and killed her, dismembered her body, then buried her parts. But something within that twelve-year-old exploded. She never quit. She never gave up. She saved her life.

Kids aren't as hung up on fear or acting "civilized" as are adults. When my children were young, I used a matter-of-fact approach with them. "These kind of people are out there and they do these kind of things." It didn't traumatize them; kids are emotionally stronger than some parents realize.

Guns and Accuracy

When pointed at you, guns are not only terrifying, they're paralyzing. That's why violent criminals use them to intimidate you into submission.

Here's some good news. Crooks don't always shoot, and when they do, they aren't very accurate. No matter how high-tech a weapon.

Under 5 percent of armed robbers actually shoot at their victims. (Knife-wielders stab or slash their victims about 21

Sgt. Don Knoll, rangemaster and director of firearms training for the San Diego Police Department, retired:

One of the biggest misconceptions about firearms concerns the very high percentage of misses that all shooters experience. That includes police officers, citizens, crooks, everyone. In police shootings, the national average is four shots fired per hit at a distance of three to nine feet. Anyone who believes it is easy to hit someone in a real-life gun battle, even at close range, has never been in a close-up gun battle.

Many people inexperienced with guns believe that a shotgun offers better protection than a handgun because of the erroneous assumption that shotgun pellets spread out at close range, thus obviating the need for accuracy — just point a shotgun in the general direction, shoot, and everyone falls. In fact, at a distance of zero to ten feet, it makes little difference if you're shot with a shotgun, rifle, or pistol, because the spread of a shotgun is very little under ten feet. A shotgun using OO buck ammunition spreads an average of one inch per yard after it is three feet beyond the barrel. So, if you're three to six feet away, a shotgun's spread is about one inch.

In some cases, the shotgun may do more damage to body tissue and cause greater trauma because of the mass which constitutes the shot plus the wadding.

But generally, from point-blank to ten feet, it doesn't make much difference what anyone is shot with. It's where your body is hit that counts. If a person is hit in a vital area— handgun, rifle, or shotgun— he or she is in trouble. If a vital spot isn't hit, and you have the will to concentrate on surviving, you probably will.

percent of the time, but fewer people die of knife wounds than of gunshot wounds.) Not only that, police departments estimate that criminals hit their target under 4 percent of the time. Earlier I said, "10 percent of armed-robbery victims are murdered." The majority of that 10 percent were executed at point-blank range.

The fact is, no one is deadly accurate under crisis conditions. But don't let that be a deciding factor for you in trying to escape a criminal with a gun. Your reason to give up your property and run should not be "He'll probably miss," but because "If I don't try, he probably won't miss."

Weapons are most often used to intimidate and control people. Most people are so intimidated they will do exactly as they are ordered.

Under any attack, you will wind up doing something or doing nothing. Facing a gun doesn't change this lousy choice. It also doesn't change the fact that whatever you do, you cannot escape risks. Do something means *escape! Run if you can!* First throw down your property, then *get away, fast!*

Doing nothing is also a choice with serious consequences. Doing nothing gives the criminal more control. Doing something—reacting immediately—works toward breaking that control. It often distracts the criminal out of his routine. He's not expecting you to react. Repeatedly, the pattern of violent crime indicates that first and immediate actions have a cumulative effect. I've seen many cases where a simple move caused the criminal to make a mistake.

I recall an armed-robbery case. Two armed men hit the owner of a small corner market. One crook was in front of the cash register. The other was with the owner, behind the register, grabbing money. The owner said, "I got the feeling the one in front of me was about to kill me, so I just ducked to the floor." The store owner's hunch was right. The crook was squeezing the trigger. When it went off, he missed the owner and killed his partner. Too bad.

Nothing happens at a crime scene the way you want it to. In some cases the victims have no chance. More often than not they do if they act quickly enough. It's creating your own luck.

The Bottom Line

1. When armed assailants shoot at fleeing victims who have willingly first given up their property, they're not just robbers, they're killers.
2. If you're hit and wounded, your best survival chances are in a public place, not the more isolated location you could end up in if you don't take the immediate risk.

Face the facts: When armed criminals are quick to shoot (a victim's handing over his property, then getting out of there, takes only seconds), the odds are he intended to shoot whatever you did. It's your decision whether to hand over the property and get out of there now . . . or hand it over and see what's next. With few exceptions, criminals will wind up doing to you whatever they've done to others.

When the armed assault is not aimed at you particularly, but the crowd you're a part of, nothing changes: get out of there immediately. For too many people, that means take cover, hide. The reason some people look for cover first instead of creating distance is that "shock boxes them in." The closer you are to the shooters, the more critical it is that you run. One reason is, most walls of buildings don't stop bullets.

Craig Randall's Story

August 7, 1982, Atlanta, Georgia. My wife and I were leaving a club near Underground Atlanta, amongst many other people. A car pulled by slowly. I remember only it was a black sedan, and . . . out of the back windows, kids, teenagers, started shooting, it was that fast. Wrong place, wrong time. Some people scattered, others tried to hide. My wife and I ran, not really knowing where we were running to at the time . . . I wanted to create distance between us and them. Suddenly I felt warmth and a stinging sensation. It didn't knock me down, it felt like a stone hit my chest. It was weird. In the furor of the moment, I just thought maybe I bumped into something. We kept running. People were shouting, screaming. The shooting was continuing.

As we got further away from the area, it felt warmer and began to be more painful. I looked down and there was blood covering my chest. My wife looked at me and screamed, "You're hit, you're hit." I yelled, "Keep running, keep running." We ducked into a nearby club. I sat down. Then the entire situation started coming down on me . . . hard. Shock started setting in. Am I going to die? What about our little boy, my wife? Then, I started coughing up blood. One of the waiters in the club was helping me, compression and stuff.

It was a .38 that hit me—collapsed one lung and tore up a couple of ribs. We were lucky . . . two teenagers in the crowd were killed. We learned later it was gang-related. The police said fifty to sixty rounds had been fired. The shooters were never caught.

I thought a lot about what we did. I mean running and not freezing up. I was a military brat. I guess I learned from my father to often ask myself, "What would I do facing a particular situation? My answer has always been simple: "Get the hell out of Dodge." I think it all came back to me with the first shot I heard.

What Craig Did Right

Everything! In my interview with Craig, it was clear: his father's influence on him as a boy to ask, "What would I do . . . ?" has become a way of life for him and his family. In fact, I met him at a training program he had brought his grown children to.

RULE #2: RESIST

When confronted by any armed criminal, your first decision is, resist or submit? There's no way out of making that first decision. Investigative officers repeatedly hear victims say, "He said he'd kill me if I didn't do what he said; I didn't have a choice." People make these desperate, hopeless statements because they truly had no other choice—in their minds. Death threats override and suppress our natural instincts of survival and we freeze up.

Submitting has consequences no less life-threatening than resisting. Submitting voluntarily places you under another's control. During many interviews with victims of rape, I've heard, "I submitted thinking that I would resist when I had a chance, but in a minute or two—it seemed like seconds—I was worse off."

Earlier you read, decide ahead of time what you fear most: injury or being controlled—psychologically and physically—by a violent criminal. If you've not yet decided, it's time. Rule #2 requires that decision.

Fear of injury boxes you in and won't allow you to be full of savage animal rage. Your mind turns you into a helpless victim, you see no recourse but to obey. Nothing can help you if you cannot get past the overwhelming terror of bodily injury.

However, if you decide your worst fear is being controlled by a violent attacker, you will have broken down the wall of fear. Note, for example, successful resistance to rape (by screaming, yelling, fighting back) comes from a mental attitude: above all, the victims who fought back feared being raped more than they feared being beaten or stabbed. Taking a hard fist to your face, taking a shot and still resisting, has zero to do with size—it's a mind-set you have for or against something.

Concentrate

In my experience teaching police officers and citizens, an obstacle to survival reactions beyond fear of injury is lack of concentration. During a life-or-death crisis, the mind tends to "float" away from the crisis at hand. This distracts you from concentrating on escape. It happens because we tend to avoid hard choices during hard times. This leaves you open to being dominated by orders from someone willing and able to kill you.

I have experienced this sensation of floating during close-to-death attacks, and so have the citizens and cops I've interviewed. They describe to me this same inability to concentrate as a major obstacle (as well as a surprise) during violence. In fact, it was this phenomenon that sparked my research into developing a survival mentality for the people I teach. Mind-setting before violence strikes helps counteract the floating sensation and helps you to concentrate during a crisis.

Immediate, Direct, Explosive

These three words—*immediate, direct, explosive*—are your guidelines to resistance. Don't wait. React immediately with full force and keep resisting. Explode! Scream! Yell! Run away! Speed off in a car.

Scream Loud and Clear

Screaming helps block out everything else and focuses you. Men and women who yell and scream have more strength, exert more force, and feel less pain because it eliminates distractions and helps you to concentrate.

But screaming is one of the most difficult physical reactions for most people. Prepare yourself simply by practicing. The best time to practice is alone in your car. You've probably already done this, but for other reasons.

Being Constrained

If the attacker is constraining you—straddling you with full weight on you, pinning you down, holding an arm around your throat, with a knife or gun to your head—shout, "Take everything." Tell him where it is—in your house, in the car, on your person. This may still be a robbery only.

If a weapon is being used against you, stabbing, slashing, shooting—you may have only seconds left. Like Steve McIntire when he grabbed the gun, or Wendy, who was being cut (and knew by looking into the man's face that he would not stop at rape), you must get the weapon off you. This most extreme situation will demand the most intense concentration on the weapon he will use to try to end your life. Grab at it. Get it in your grip; at least get it out of his. To put it bluntly, it's a fight for the weapon. I've said it previously: lousy choices are all you are left with when you're constrained and cannot immediately escape. Do nothing while he's stabbing or shooting you or another, or grab at the weapon to get it off you.

If the attacker is trying to move you, he cannot stay in the same position (straddling you, keeping you in a chokehold, pressing a knife against you) for very long. The initial controlling position will quickly change and will continue to change, which is likely to give you a slightly better opportunity to resist and escape. This very issue is coming up in the next story. Kathleen Sullivan was first straddled and her face pushed into the mud, held down by the full body weight of a knife-wielding man twice her size on her. Yet one slight movement by her altered his position slightly, which gave her a break that she made work for her, eventually to the point of escaping him.

Unarmed Assault

This book is primarily about armed violence. This section is about unarmed violence. When he's close to you and you have to fight back physically, keep it simple. You won't have time to do anything fancy or choreographed.

Gouge the Eyes

Against an unarmed attacker who is punching you in the face, choking you, the simplest and most effective resistance is to gouge his eyes. Kneeing him in the groin is okay, nothing wrong with biting, but gouging the eyes works best.

When you have only split seconds, gouging at the eyes is your best bet because they are the most sensitive body part, requiring the least force from you. You don't even have to touch someone's eyes to produce a reflexive movement.

Furthermore, concentrating 100 percent of your mental and physical power on one objective is far more effective than splitting your concentration by trying different moves. Anyone who practices optional moves in a gym, trying to determine which one works best, is kidding himself, because no one has time to weigh options at a crime scene when being choked or hit in the face.

When we taught men and women police officers how to arrest and control, we instructed them in fifty-one pain-compliance-type martial-arts holds. But when it came to surviving an attempt against their life and a weapon was not available, it was "go for the eyes and trachea."

Women are usually the target of unarmed attackers because men are perceived as more physically powerful. Slightly under 80 percent of the men who attack women do so unarmed. The reverse is true of men who attack men. In fact, women can be just as effective and dangerous as men close in because no strength factor is involved in gouging the eyes, biting, or crushing the trachea.

I said *gouge* the eyes (fingers and thumb straight and rigid)—not poke or jab with one or two fingers. Don't worry about perfection, just get something on the end of your hand in his eye.

It's disgusting to think about gouging someone's eyes, even a complete stranger who is attacking you. When I discuss this tactic during rape training, I can see a wall going up in some of the participants' eyes. If you're too civilized to envision yourself maiming another human being, or if you have difficulty believing that another human being can be a sadistic, brutal torturer and killer with no conscience whatsoever, you will mentally doom your efforts to survive.

Think about this instead: you would do *anything* to protect your child; you wouldn't hesitate to gouge out an assailant's eyes. That's the primitive rage you need to keep in touch with.

Take a lesson from one animal in particular. When a cat is cornered by a dog, the cat is usually outweighed fivefold or more. What does that cat do? He goes for the dog's face and eyes. Cats never go for a dog's groin or kneecap. Mine has never lost a fight with a dog.

With an unarmed attacker, the odds are high he'll be choking you from behind. You will have very little time to react. If your windpipe is being choked from behind (with an arm across your trachea), you have less than split seconds because the trachea is easily crushed. If the pressure is on the side of your neck, the blood to your brain is constricted and you will lose consciousness in four to eight seconds. Forget fancy flips and going for the groin. These moves may work in gyms or on television and movie screens, but they don't often work in real life. Your last and best chance in these extreme conditions is to reach back for the eyes with both hands and gouge. Impossible! You can't do it! I've heard young police-officers-to-be voice the same uncertainty. The answer for them is the same as for you. You can, especially when your alternative is to do nothing while he chokes the air from you. Always go for the eyes. Immediate, direct, explosive. It's the one move that will work best for you against unarmed attackers.

Biting

Bite a chunk out of his cheek, nose, or neck. I know these explanations and pictures I'm placing in your mind are ugly. Remember, you must be as uncivilized as he is for a few seconds in order to escape. Okay, you can't imagine yourself biting into a human being's cheek, nose, lip. Compare the grossness of biting into flesh against what lies ahead. Pound for pound of square-inch power, nothing matches your jaw.

I remember my first biting case, in 1967. An eighteen-year-old Laundromat attendant was locking up when a man forced his way in, locked the door, and dragged her in a chokehold to the back area. Shoving her up against the wall, with both hands against her shoulders, his first move was to force a deep, tongue-into-her-mouth kiss. She bit down hard and severed it at the halfway point. That ended his attack fast. We got him in the emergency room. The crime report read, *attempted* rape, not rape. Big difference.

Should you bite a man who is forcing you to orally copulate him? I'll answer that this way: I would in a second! I won't guarantee the violence will be over, but the forced oral copulation will be over.

Another biting case involved a fifty-eight-year-old woman who worked as a cocktail-lounge waitress. She left at closing time, around 2 A.M., and a patron forced his way into her car at knifepoint. He drove her car, holding her down and next to him. They were on Interstate 8, a major freeway going through San Diego, going 55 mph in the center lane. Knife in hand, he forced her to orally copulate him while driving her to a more isolated location. She bit down with everything she had (no, she didn't bite it off). The car wound up off the freeway, up the embankment, and crashed. He ran off, she ran in the opposite direction. A few minutes later, cops found her a block away from the crash, hiding and trembling, with minor injuries, but not raped. We went to the nearest emergency room. Sure enough, a man was being treated for a deep penile bite wound.

If I could change one thing about how society addresses the differences between men and women, it would be how families here and in other countries bring up little boys and little girls. Little boys aren't told to suffer abuse or insult, or to submit because we don't want them to be hurt. Instead, little boys are given a pat on the back for being ''brave,'' and they grow up prepared to defend themselves and their families, mentally and physically. If their fathers have ever had to protect themselves or others, the stories are told like a badge of honor until the families can repeat them word for word. The lesson boys learn is they can fight back and be brave like dad.

Little girls, on the other hand, often grow up with more submissive expectations, and the message is, ''Don't make someone angry enough to hurt you.'' Many girls grow up afraid of doing anything that might get them hurt, and they become easy prey for abusive men. Not only that, if their mothers have ever been assaulted or raped, whether by a stranger or an acquaintance, they remain silent for fear of upsetting their children. Yet a mother's story, whatever the outcome, can be the most powerful teaching tool.

Of course we don't have proof that fighting back will work in every case, any more than there's proof that submission will work in every case. There is proof, however, for every case when a victim did nothing and was injured, there are countless cases when victims did nothing and were *not* killed or seriously wounded.

Nonconfrontation tactics work for law enforcement, who have the power of backup and other officers essential for a wait-and-let-it-defuse approach. A woman being stuffed into the backseat of a car doesn't have backup help, nor does she have any time to wait it out.

Begging and pleading don't work because if the criminal had any compassion, he wouldn't be attacking you in the first place. Worse yet, begging and pleading rob you of precious time. Violent criminals are habitual, hardened criminals who have worked their way up from lesser to more serious crimes.

Resist by concentrating everything—physically, emotionally, mentally—to fight off physical and mental control of you. Tap into your uncivilized, primitive rage . . . it's there, I have it and you have it.

Kathleen Sullivan's Story

October 6, 1986. I had decided to go for a walk after lunch in a nice neighborhood in San Diego, a hilly area with a walking path frequently used by joggers, bicyclists, and walkers. Unfortunately, not this time. I was wearing headphones—just walking along and listening to music.

There was no warning. The initial strike took only a couple of seconds. It happened so fast, I was in shock— almost paralyzed. He had hit me from behind with his full body weight. The force catapulted both of us down a hillside. He slammed my face into the dirt and mud. My mind began to race. It flashed through me: "Save yourself. He's going to rape you." I felt so terribly alone.

He was kneeling on top of my neck and shoulders, pushing my face into the dirt, covering my mouth and my nose, choking me with the other hand. I couldn't see, couldn't move. I was pinned down. He yelled at me, "Don't scream! Don't move, and you won't be hurt!" Terror gripped me. I couldn't believe this was happening to me, that I had no warning.

I was afraid he would choke me unconscious. At first, that was my main concern. I purposely went completely limp. When I did that, he released the pressure around my face and my neck. Then my first chance came. He moved his body slightly off my shoulders. I flipped over, surprised at my strength. He was terrifying. A nylon stocking covered his face.

I have to say it again, the feeling of being all alone was overpowering. I remember thinking my family would want me to fight. But something else was the driving force for me: fear of being raped. I had to fight against being raped. The survival class cemented that for me.

I was screaming. He screamed back, "Shut up!" I got louder. It really bothered him. The struggle was not going the way he expected. He seemed shocked at my resistance. He couldn't control me. I was a wild, crazy, screaming woman. He was getting nowhere.

Fighting didn't stop my fear. I was terrified, but fighting did make me stronger. I am five feet three inches and weigh 115 pounds, but I was mad as hell, determined to stop him.

Then he pulled out a knife. It sent me up to a higher level of terror and hate. I didn't care if I got cut up. I was not going to be raped. That decision helped. I knew if he got the knife next to my throat, it would be worse for me, so I grabbed the blade. People have asked me, "Was it a hard decision to make—to grab a knife blade?" It happened so fast that I just did what I felt I had to do. That knife enraged me. It made me feel that this man was truly determined to cut me up, maybe kill me, and that rape was just one of the things he planned to do to me. I decided he was not going to have an easy time.

I remember focusing all my thoughts, all my power, on that knife blade. We were both desperately fighting over it. He was having a hard time holding on to his own knife. He kept saying, "I'll cut you. I'll cut you."

That son of a bitch was already cutting me. There was blood everywhere. That just made me more angry and terrified.

Suddenly everything seemed to turn. I had become the aggressor. I could feel it, and I sensed that he knew it, too.

I was making everything go wrong for him. I think he was afraid someone would hear, so he put one hand back onto my face to muffle my screams. The other hand was still holding his knife.

Then it happened—one of his fingers pushed into my mouth. I clamped down on that finger with everything I had. My jaws locked. "You're going to pay, you bastard," went through my mind so distinctly. He froze, he was not looking at me anymore, he was looking at his finger. He couldn't pull it out. I had a death grip on it. He yelled, "I'm outta here!" I was so enraged, I bit down more, as hard as I could. I actually felt my teeth go through his bone. My whole mouth filled with blood. I gagged and spit it all out. That's when he got away. He pulled back, stood up holding his hand, looking at it. He never looked at me again.

Looking back, I was so enraged that I went primal. When he threatened to kill me with that knife, I believed him. That helped me to fight. Being so afraid and hating him helped me. It gave me strength. Biting—I guess there is something animalistic about it. It sure works.

I believe the most important factor in my escaping that

assault was making a decision ahead of time, what I stand for and what I stand against. The only one who can make the decision to fight back—to resist—is you. You're responsible for making your own chances.

Also, I think it is so important to know it doesn't matter if you try but can't stop him, as long as you have tried. I think it is psychologically important to resist. Resisting protects you physically now, and psychologically later.

I was injured, but I expected that. I was cut immediately and badly, but I didn't let that stop me. I remember thinking, "Raping me will be the hardest thing you have ever done in your life." I hated him for what he was trying to do to me.

Everything I had thought about regarding rape clicked in. I learned in our training program, "That's falling back on training."

I also learned something else from that attack: Just because I'm a woman doesn't mean I can't fight like an animal. Women will fight like animals to protect their children. You have to get mentally crazy so that nothing is beyond you. Somehow you have to transfer the fear of what he is doing to you to hate and anger against him. Add primal animal instincts to that anger. It sure helps. As far as biting down on his finger, I still get a horrible feeling in my mouth when I think about it. Sometimes I have to think, "Did it really happen?" But I don't mind remembering what I did, because I did it right.

What Kathleen Did Right

She decided she feared rape more than she feared injury, then made a bottom-line decision: "Raping me will be the hardest thing a man ever does."

She made that decision because she did not shield herself from the harsh realities of rape. That enabled her to concentrate on resisting and not the paralyzing fear of injuries. Decisions like these that Kathleen made (and Wendy—story earlier in this book) are pivotal decisions in women's lives. And they should be — men have those kinds of decisions for their lives.

For the Record

Kathleen still walks in the area where she was attacked. She says, "Yes, the area brings back memories, but I refuse to let that bastard change my life."

The man who attempted to rape Kathleen was never caught. The investigating officer told her, "Losing the finger will not stop him . . . maybe for a while, but he'll be back to rape again. They always do."

"How do I know resistance doesn't escalate things?" In my experience, escalation due to resistance is the exception, not the rule. Anyone with a gun or knife is a recidivist, and it's much more likely that you have escalated nothing.

According to Paul Pfingst, district attorney of San Diego County, in words repeated over and over by other officers of the criminal justice system: "Resisting doesn't make it worse—that's what I've learned in every kind of case involving violence, including murder cases. Few violent criminals have any more than a dim understanding of what form of violence they plan against a victim. Because what they do versus what they cannot do is largely dictated by what their victim does or does not do in the first few seconds."

A criminal who has progressed to violent crimes has established a pattern of behavior. Victims who submit and fit into his pattern will be nothing more than *next*. If he's a rapist, he will rape you. If his pattern includes ramming foreign objects into women, he'll do it to you. If he's a robber who shoots or stabs his victims, that won't change for you. One thing that will make you different from his other victims and change the outcome is your explosive resistance.

The bottom line: Resist. When violent people are in control, the crimes always get worse, especially at crime scene #2. For the first few crucial seconds, be driven by the primitive rage that is in all of us. We must cast aside our civilized side when up against violence.

RULE #3: CRIME SCENE #2

Murder is one thing, but torture, mayhem, and savagery—it takes more time for these crimes. Every torture case I have prosecuted involved a victim isolated and completely controlled.

—PAUL PFINGST, SAN DIEGO DA

You've read the stats on violent criminals. If a guy is going to shoot or rape you in public, what will he do to you at crime scene #2? As I said before, time only works against you, and the place of first contact is as good as it's going to get. You have options, chances, there. But if you're moved from crime scene #1 (first contact), your options and chances disappear. You may be moved only five feet from the sidewalk to the other side of some bushes, or fifteen feet down into a ravine. You may be moved only a few feet, or miles. The sole purpose in moving you is to get you out of sight and reduce the chance of intervention. You wind up isolated and at the mercy of the merciless. A crime scene #2 investigation usually involves murder, rape, sometimes sadism and torture.

Never allow the attacker to move you to a more isolated spot (behind the wall, over to the hedge). If he's only a robber, he doesn't need to move you. A rapist and some killers are looking for isolation, seclusion. Risk everything to stop a criminal from moving you to crime scene #2. Risk injury. Risk being shot. Lousy options now are better than no options later.

People ask me, "With a gun at my head, arm around my throat, should I risk screaming?" Yes. You can remain silent and do what he says or make it difficult for him and try to escape. Go dead weight, hold on to something, making it even more difficult for him to drag you. Anyone so determined to move you is not just a robber.

Crash It!

Most crimes of abduction or kidnapping of men, women, or children of any age involve a motor vehicle. Consider these stories, which are unfortunately commonplace. They only warranted a newspaper back-page, short column.

Story 1: ". . . two high school girls, kidnapped by a man posing as a law enforcement officer. With one in the backseat and one in the front, he drove to a remote area where he raped both girls."

Story 2: ". . . a woman, kidnapped at gunpoint. The man emerged from the backseat armed with a gun and a knife, ordered her to drive to a deserted area where he raped her."

Story 3: "An elderly man, waiting in his car while his wife shopped nearby, was confronted by two men. One had a gun. They forced their way into his car and ordered him to drive to a deserted sand quarry. After robbing him, they ordered him to kneel. While he prayed and begged for his life, they executed him, then drove off with his car." (Cops find out what happened at grisly crime scenes when criminals testify against each other or cop a plea in exchange for leniency.)

If you're abducted while driving your car or are forced into their car, *crash it.* It's the best and usually the only way to give yourself a second and last chance. Don't wait until you're going 50 mph, and don't drive around looking for a police car or something ideal to hit. Crash it at 10,

15 mph, immediately into another parked car in the parking lot, trash Dumpster, fire hydrant. Don't be picky, just crash it.

Don't waste time, and maybe your one chance, trying to grab the steering wheel, screaming out the window, honking the horn, or driving erratically to get the attention of law enforcement. Nothing works as effectively as crashing the car when you need help because:

1. Nothing else will create as much noise, commotion, and attention as a crash.
2. Nothing else will put as much pressure on him to get out and away.

To be an extremely difficult victim and avoid crime scene #2, crash it.

When you're driving, crashing the car is fairly simple. Except that crashing contradicts everything you've been trained to do. Overcome that wall by mentally picturing yourself crashing your car, with your family in it if need be.

"If I crash, will my insurance cover it?" is a question I'm sometimes asked. My answer is always, I don't know. But I can say this: in my family, whether or not our car insurance covers one of my daughters purposely crashing her car to escape an abduction is of zero concern to me.

America's new breed of monster criminals are not deterred from violence because children are present. January 19, 1993, Eustis, Florida: A young mother with her two little girls, ages three and six, were confronted at gunpoint walking to their car in a shopping-mall parking lot. The four minors forced her to drive them to a woodsy area. The one with the gun executed the two little girls and wounded the mother. Then all four took turns raping the mother. She survived, if there is such a condition as surviving after a crime like that. At gunpoint, in a shopping-mall parking lot—crashing the car was her only chance and a damn good one to change the outcome.

If you're not the driver, it's tougher but still possible. Force the abductor to crash it. Don't be constrained by your civilized mind-set and think in terms of grabbing the steering wheel or reaching for the ignition key or stepping on the gas pedal that he controls. These strategies are too civilized to be successful. Instead, *gouge his eyes!* Ugly, but your best bet to cause a crash.

If you're in the backseat and controlled by others, you have only seconds before you're overpowered and forced to the floor. Don't waste these seconds fighting against the men next to you in your frantic effort to get back out (in the confines of the backseat, they will overpower you even more easily than they did outside). Don't grab for the door handle (the men's bulk alone will thwart your efforts). Your last-ditch chance in the fleeting seconds ahead is to try to force the driver to crash. Even trying to get to the driver will require a superhuman effort, but he's the one who will move you to crime scene #2. Go for the driver's eyes, it's your last chance.

With any kidnapping—political, religious, grudge, extortion, robbery, rape, by novice or professional; it doesn't matter what the reasons are—there are limited ways to accomplish and limited ways to stop the crime. Forcing a crash (right away) is your most sure method.

Whether he's a professional or "street crook," his first move against you will be difficult to stop because it's seldom anticipated and usually the last thing you expect. But you can stop him from moving you to an isolated spot. *Crash it!* It's a crucial crime-survival decision because it prevents the end of the line for you: crime scene #2.

Bob Ring, the thirty-five-year veteran detective quoted earlier:

She was a twenty-seven-year-old, married, from a small Southern community, visiting relatives in San Diego. One evening she decided to take a walk about 7 P.M. Six or seven outlaw bikers grabbed her from the street, hit her numerous times, then one of them forced her onto the back of his motorcycle and they all took off. It's not uncommon for outlaw bikers and street gangs to abduct women from the street and take them to their clubhouse to share.

They took her to an abandoned trailer where more bikers were partying, stripped her, and tied her spread-eagle on the couch. Then everyone lined up . . . twelve to fifteen outlaw bikers took their turns. They burned her forehead with cigarettes more than a dozen times. This went on for five hours—tied down and gang-raped—one of my worst cases. I think her mental state shut down because later it was difficult to get some of the details about everything they did to her.

This young woman's only chance went by fast. She would have had to force that motorcycle down on the freeway. She could have done that, but she would have been seriously hurt. That's the kind of decision many victims are faced with. Nothing is going to be easy or injury-free. People need to know that.

That poor woman had no way of knowing what was ahead of her. Crimes always get worse in isolated places. Any cop can tell you, when outlaw bikers or gang members abduct you, they're going to take you to an isolated area, and it will be long and horrible.

Some people wonder how often outlaw bikers and street gangs abduct women off the street. When I joined the San Diego police in 1966, I was shocked to learn that gangs, whether outlaw bikers or inner-city gangs, actually abducted women—teenagers to forty-year-olds—off the street for all-night gang parties. The woman would be tied, chained, or handcuffed to the four corners of a filthy bed and then raped in every conceivable fashion—sodomized, forced to orally copulate, foreign objects forced into her vagina—by drunken, drugged-up gang members. I've seen seasoned and hardened cops sickened from these cases . . . and I've been among them.

It is difficult to determine the frequency of such crimes because many women refuse to go through the criminal justice system, which forces them to relive the experience in order to testify. Those who do report such cases often have little specific recall because their minds naturally shut down during the incident. These cases happen, but few reach court or the newspapers for these reasons.

Catherine Dunlap's Story

Atlanta, Georgia. April 26, 1991. I was twenty-four, working in outside sales for a temporary labor pool putting people to work.

I was leaving work and it had started to rain. I saw one of the laborers outside the labor pool. He asked me for a ride down the street to get his check cashed. He was very reliable, one of our A-rated workers. I hesitated, even though he'd been in my car a dozen times before when I had taken him to job sites. Something in my gut said, "Not a good idea." I felt uneasy about his request. Not scared, just uneasy. I was fairly street-smart and still let it happen.

He was so nice the way he asked, I didn't have the heart to say no. We passed several minimarts where he could have cashed his check. He kept saying, "No, not this one, the next one." I asked, "Which one are we going to?" and he said, "It's right around the corner." "Well, this is the last one," I told him.

Suddenly, he pulled out a knife. The blade seemed so

long, probably six inches. Immediately, he said, "I'll kill you if you don't do exactly what I say." He reached over and put his hand on my knee. It was almost like he was trying to calm me or something. It was really strange. I was trying to talk him out of it. "Why are you doing this? Tommy is expecting me home and we're going grocery shopping. I'll just let you out here. You can take the car."

He said, "Just shut up and drive. Get to the interstate." Whenever I tried to talk, he would tell me to shut up or he was going to cut my head off. He kept saying that a lot.

About this time it started raining pretty hard; it was nearly six-thirty and getting dark. I was asking questions: "Do you want to get out here? Do you want me to take you home? Do you live up here?" I know it sounds naive of me, but I think I expected that surely he would change his mind.

God, I was scared. In shock really. I was trying to think of a way to get him or me out of my car peacefully. Something! Oddly enough, almost immediately as soon as I got on the interstate, I thought about wrecking my car. But I didn't have the guts to do it or the right opportunity.

I was shaking terribly. Suddenly he said, "Get off the road." We'd been on I-20 traveling eastbound, and we were pretty far out of Atlanta. There was a light as soon as I exited, and a car waiting for the signal. I was so tempted to have a wreck with that car, but I was worried there could be a child in it. I just didn't have the nerve to do it. It must not have been desolate enough for him—he made me get back on the interstate in the opposite direction. All of a sudden, he started to become violent. Cussing a lot, fondling my leg, moving higher on my leg toward my lap. It's almost unbelievable to me how terrified I was and how difficult it was for me to think straight.

He was getting real nervous because the rain was coming down hard and I was driving really slow. I kept thinking, "Maybe someone will see this as unusual. Maybe someone will do something to help me." A lot of silly things go through your mind at a time like this.

I was hoping someone would intervene. I kept looking around for a cop. "Keep your eyes on the road, just drive, damn it, just drive," he would warn. He was monitoring me so closely. There was really no way I could do anything without him knowing. I even tried to go to the bathroom on myself; I was getting desperate. I thought that would gross him out enough to leave me alone, but I couldn't do it. We kept on driving and he really started fondling my genitals and ripping my panty hose. I was clinching my legs real tight. This is what really haunts me a lot; he kept saying, "Open your legs, open your fucking legs or I'm going to kill you and cut your damn head off." Every time he threatened me he flashed his knife in front of my face.

I could identify him and he knew it. There was no doubt in my mind at this point that I was going to be raped and then killed; he was practically raping me in the car with his hands anyway.

Finally, I realized I had to wreck my car. It was my only chance. But I didn't see anything to hit. By this time, I was far out of Atlanta, and my best chance to crash was gone. If I'd wrecked it earlier, I would have saved myself lots of grief. The further we got away from town, the worse it got; cussing, touching me, it was horrible.

I passed one exit, but there was nothing to hit, then another. It was a rural area; I passed two more exits, maybe more. I was desperate to crash. I knew that it was my last shot at living through this.

Then I saw the exit for Douglasville. I was traveling at about 55 mph, a little slower than interstate speed because of the rain. I saw activity at the exit: a gas station, Waffle House. I held tight to the wheel, looked out the rearview mirror, and floored it. I crossed two lanes of traffic in absolutely no time at all. My arms were gripping the steering wheel so tightly. He grabbed the steering wheel and tried to turn it back to the left. He screamed, "Don't kill me, I'll let you go." I think I said something like, "Yeah, right, you bastard." I hated him, the son of a bitch. He was big enough to overpower me, but there was no way he could get that steering wheel back to the left. I was so strong at that moment, I couldn't believe it. I did what I had to do.

Actually, what I tried to do was hit a tree on his side. I wanted to kill him. For sure, I didn't want to hit my side. The ramp was slick and I didn't have that much control because he was grabbing it, too. I ended up hitting a green exit sign, then I spun around and hit a tree with the front of my car. I didn't hit where I planned on crashing, but I crashed real good. Probably 40 mph. My car was totaled. Just before we hit, I can remember, he was braced looking straight ahead, screaming, "Don't kill me." He still had the knife, but not on me.

Fortunately, I always wear my seat belt. That son of a bitch wasn't strapped in.

The last thing I remember was seeing him get out of the car and run. I ran the other way screaming bloody murder into the traffic that was coming down the exit ramp.

A lady in a pickup truck pulled up and said something like, "Get in, get in. What happened to you?" I was hysterical at this point. I just screamed, "Rape!" That still affects me when I think about how close it was and how I went from being a self-sufficient and secure person to hysterical. I couldn't talk. I just screamed over and over, "Rape, rape!"

She pulled into a gas station to call the police. I locked her door. I was still hysterical, still screaming. I ripped off what was left of my panty hose, threw them on the floorboard, and started stomping on them, screaming the whole time.

Some people ask if I was afraid of dying when I decided to crash the car. I didn't want to die, but I didn't want him to have his way with me and then be murdered. I do remember thinking, "If nothing else, at least this way I have some control." Once I decided to crash, I was on track. That's all I thought about.

It was a difficult decision, but it was the right thing to do and the only thing to do. It was my last chance. I would change one thing, though, if it ever happens again; I won't wait so long.

What Catherine Did Wrong

Catherine ignored her first gut feelings. Then she tried to negotiate and talk him into changing his mind. She worried about finding the right place to crash her car.

What Catherine Did Right

Unlike most victims, Catherine made common mistakes and got a second chance. When she began to concentrate only on escape, "crashing it" became her uncompromisable goal.

For the Record

Catherine's attacker had a prior criminal record. He was apprehended, convicted, and is still in prison. I believe he intended to rape her, then murder her. He had to; he's a recidivist and she could identify him.

In introspective moments at isolated crime scenes, I have looked at corpses and wondered, If he or she could have foreseen the future, would they have risked everything where they were first attacked? Any criminal knows that whatever his first crime is— armed assault, bank robbery— by moving a victim or hostage in any way, it's kidnapping, and he now faces a capital offense—which could carry the death penalty. For him, there is no advantage to letting victims live.

The bottom line: First contact (crime scene #1), the situation is dangerous and very likely life-threatening, too. At crime scene #2, it's near hopeless and the end of your line.

RULE #4: NEVER, NEVER GIVE UP

Near the end of his life, Winston Churchill delivered the commencement address at a British university. Physically infirm, he had to be helped to the podium. He clung to the podium for a long time, gazing down. Finally he raised his head, and the voice that years before had called Britain back from the brink of destruction sounded publicly for the last time in history:

"Never give up. Never give up. Never give up."

Churchill turned and returned to his seat unassisted. After a silence, the entire audience, as one, rose to applaud the man who had held the nation together during its most fateful hour.

The words *never give up,* so often repeated to us as children, are fundamental to everything we achieve in our lives. They are also the most important words in every officer survival training program. They are no less important in a citizen survival training program. They are the words that begin and end every person's fight to survive.

On the night before Christmas Eve, 1976, gangs tried to "off" two Los Angeles deputy sheriffs. Mike Waters was one of them, and ever since, California Law Enforcement Survival Training has used his story as an example of what it takes to stay alive.

Mike Waters's Story

December 23, 1976, Los Angeles. My partner George and I were working a gang detail out of the Firestone Station. Two gangs, a party—we were expecting trouble. Cruising the area, we saw three males walking down Florence Avenue who appeared to be gang members but weren't known to us. Later we learned that two were active gang members and recent parolees. They were training the third guy in armed robberies.

We stopped and called out that we wanted to talk to them. While we were still in the car, they suddenly hesitated with their backs to us, then spun around, all together. They started walking toward us fast—three abreast. I got a cold, panicked feeling; I knew something was going down.

Then they split up. One came toward me, two went toward George on the other side of our car. They were ten feet off the front of the hood. I had one foot out of the car. Damn! We were losing control of the "stop." The two on George's side charged and jumped him.

About the same instant, the guy coming at me pulled his hand out of his pocket. I saw a flash—heard a pop. Something hit my eye. There was nothing but bright lights in front of me everywhere. God, I've been shot in the eye! Everything went into slow motion. I could see his face, but blurry. Pop! Pop! Still shooting at me. I was staggering, trying to stay on my feet. I was fighting it, but I couldn't seem to stop falling backward. Pop! Pop! Shit! Still firing at me. I hit the pavement on my face—like a watermelon. Another pop. He was still shooting. I was hurt bad. I knew it was over.

I couldn't believe I'd been shot. I'm a peace officer—a damn good one. How the hell could this happen?

Christmas was in two days. My little girl. It wasn't right. I was thinking all this and I wasn't paying attention to what was happening. My mind was drifting . . . the whole thing was taking forever. God, I was hoping he would go away! Just go away. At that point, I was giving up. The worst thing to do and I was doing it.

All of a sudden, he was on my back. Then his gun was to the back of my head. I knew what was next, but I still wasn't fighting back. I was paralyzed—too stunned. Click! Click! Click! I will never forget that sound: the most beautiful sound in the world. Then he began beating me on the top of my head. It took twenty stitches to close it up.

Finally, I snapped back. I could feel the rage coming over me. I remember thinking, "I've taken a hit in the eye. I'm dead. I'm taking this bastard with me. I'm taking him out." I pushed myself up and backhanded him with a left to his face. Knocked him off-balance. My strength was unbelievable. I got to my knees, drew, and fired one round, hitting him in the side. It didn't knock him down. By that time, I was up—we were three feet apart. His gun was aimed at my gut—my gun aimed at his gut. Click, click, click . . . he was still empty.

I had a full load. For me, it was bang! bang! bang! But I was missing him. Everything was so blurry. Blood all over me, lights still flashing in front of me. Everything was almost pure white. I leveled toward his chest and fired once. Hit him dead center. He went down—dead.

I looked for George and rushed to the rear of our car. One guy was on George, beating him. He looked up and we were eyeball-to-eyeball. I pushed my gun out in front and got him between the eyes. Two down—one to go. Click! Click! Click! Damn, I was out of ammunition. Instantly, George rolled over and started firing, too.

I half-stumbled, half-crawled to my car radio and

screamed, "We've been shot! Request immediate assistance!" I gave them our location. I remember being so scared because I was bleeding so badly. I was dying— I knew it.

We could hear the sirens—great sound. Suddenly, one of our units screeched to a halt in front of the bank. Great feeling seeing him roll up . . .

After I was up and around, I gave a lot of instruction in officer survival based on what we did right and wrong. At first, we gave up because it seemed easier to quit. Thank God we snapped out of it. Survival was possible only if we fought back. We knew that.

George once told me, "The lectures in the police academy flashed through my mind—don't give up, fight back." It's like Strong and I and others say, the training takes over.

George and I gave them the advantage by making mistakes, and crooks will always take advantage of a mistake. In prison exercise yards, crooks practice taking cops and citizens out. I've seen films of inmates practicing escape and control moves, even how-to-kill moves.

The thing that snapped me back to reality was that the dirtbag continued attacking me, hitting me; I got mad, enraged. That's what I needed.

What pulls a cop through is the same as what will pull a citizen through. Not a damn bit of difference. You've got to overcome thinking about how badly you're hurt. I took a round in the kill zone, my eye socket. Every doctor I've talked to says I should be dead. Don't believe it. No matter how bad you're hurt, you can't quit. Not giving up is the only chance of survival.

If you quit under attack, you're his, bought and paid for. But if you try, there's hope. It's a little like being a kid fighting on the school grounds. The bully hits you in the nose. You hurt, you bleed. If you do nothing, the bully will hit you twenty more times. The difference is, against the bully on the playground, you lose the fight. If you quit against a crook, you lose for good.

Something else I think is important: fighting back stops the pain. I know that for a fact. When I was fighting to survive that night, I didn't feel anything, but when it was over and I was in the back of the patrol car headed for the hospital, then I felt the pain . . . lots of it.

What Mike Did Wrong

Mike got a gut feeling and put it aside. That placed him and George too deep into it to back off. I've made that same mistake; when cops and citizens ignore gut fears, many of them pay the price.

What Mike Did Right

He snapped out of the common ''give-up'' response. Only then did his rage and anger replace fear of dying.

For the Record

Mike regained his eyesight but was badly beaten a few years later and forced to retire. His partner George was gunned down a couple of years later in a separate incident.

When everything is on the line, every man and woman has a storehouse of power available to use. You only have to aim everything you have—mental and physical—at escape. The power follows. If you are ever the next target, your only chance to escape, and maybe to survive, will depend on your resolve to never, never give up. Attitude makes a helluva difference.

I still remember this phone call, February 1985: "Lisa May, who took your survival program, was attacked. She's in the hospital, hurt, but alive. She asked me to let you know."

I went to the hospital the next day. Lisa's head was covered in bandages—just her face showing. Both hands were covered with bandages, too—every finger was broken. But she was all smiles.

Her first words were, "I stopped him. He didn't rape me, he didn't kill me."

When I left, Lisa, still smiling, said, "I'm so happy, it could have been real bad."

Lisa May's Story

January 31, 1985. I was making trips back and forth from the laundry room, which was in a building back near the alley. A guy asked for directions and I gave them. He acted a little weird, but I didn't think much about it.

When I returned to the laundry room, the door was closed. I thought, "I didn't leave the door closed—that's odd." I opened the door and noticed the light was off. I thought I'd left it on; I always do. I reached to flip the switch, but it was already up, so I figured the light had burned out. I walked in. Suddenly, something slammed into my head and the door shut!

The first blow stunned me. Before I could comprehend what was happening, it was followed by another and another. He was hitting me with a four-foot steel post used for barbed-wire fencing. He was baseball-swinging that steel post; every blow just shattered through me. I put my hands on top of my head to try to protect it. I could feel my finger bones splintering with every blow to my head. I tried to scream, but nothing came out. I felt paralyzed.

It happened so fast. But the blows seemed so slow, almost as if I was watching it happen to me, like a movie. I started to give up. I covered my head and prayed I would survive. So many things were running through my mind. I thought of my son, Ryan, and how I might never see him again. I remember thinking after it was over how difficult it was initially to concentrate—we had been told it would be difficult, but I was shocked how much so.

"My God, he's trying to kill me. Why?" That flashed through my mind.

Then I remembered, "Fight! Go for the face!" I screamed. My instincts were finally taking hold. He shouted, "Shut up!" I first thought, "Okay, okay." I thought, "If I do what he says, he'll stop hitting me." But then something in me yelled, "Fight!" I screamed again. Sometimes I could scream; sometimes nothing would come out. The fear, the terror, is probably the most overwhelming thing to overcome. It's paralyzing.

I reached deep inside, forcing myself to scream. That did it. I didn't stop screaming, kicking, or striking at him. He kept baseball-swinging that steel post at my head. It seemed like forever. It didn't stop. Then I could feel anger and hate come over me. He was trying to take me from my family. That was the turning point for me. I hated him. It was so weird—I could almost feel power building up in me. Suddenly, he stopped, turned around, opened the door, looked out, and ran.

I got up and ran home. I didn't realize how badly I was hurt. I didn't feel anything. When I got to our front door, I took my hands from my head. Each hand looked like a deformed club. My fingers were smashed and twisted, and most with bone sticking out of them. I kicked at our door. I was covered in blood. I'll never forget the look on Bill's face when he opened the door. Ryan started screaming, "Mommy! Mommy!"

Thank God, I finally got mad. That's when I snapped out of my shock. Once I began fighting, I didn't stop, nor did I feel any pain. You have to be angry at what is happening to you to get over the fear and terror of it all. And hating people like him helps. You must believe that what an attacker starts out doing is only the beginning. I remembered Sanford Strong saying, "If you fear being hurt by fighting back, you're doomed." Now I know it's true. I used to say how lucky I was. Now, I know I made my own luck.

It happens so fast. If you're ever attacked, I want to tell you, there will be millions of things running through your mind. You have got to snap out of it and get back to what is going on at that moment. You must get rid of everything in your mind that doesn't count and concentrate on what you must do.

What I found out later was scary. He was a seventeen-year-old kid and had attacked two other women.

He attacked one after knocking on her front door and telling her he was sick and wanted to call his mother. She let him in and got some soda crackers for him. He took a knife from her kitchen and stabbed her in the face, for no reason. He killed another woman by putting a pillowcase over her head and beating her to death. No reason.

What Lisa May Did Wrong

Lisa May ignored her gut instincts about her attacker and his demeanor. Then ignored the door, the light; she talked herself out of worrying.

What Lisa May Did Right

Although she initially gave up, she snapped out of it. Lisa said it well: "Believing what he's doing is just the beginning and hating him helps."

For the Record

Bottom-line survival decisions must never exclude hate and anger, not at just what he's doing, but at him directly. Superhuman, animal-type strength is always rooted in our strongest of emotions, hate and fear.

Lisa May recovered fully, without any deformities. She has spoken eloquently on national television programs about what a woman must do to survive. Her teenage attacker was charged, tried, and freed because of a series of investigative blunders (lost evidence, etc.) and because additional victims refused to return for further trials.

Survival training is based on a fundamental understanding: surviving criminal violence is not determined by numbers, size, gender, better armament; it requires an individual's concentration on and commitment to survival decisions. At crime scenes, some things are beyond our control, but limiting the violence is within our power. Escaping and limiting injuries requires a split-second mental shift from an every-day-as-usual routine to an immediate life-saving reaction.

I've asked you to adopt a law enforcement officer's survival mind-set. You don't need to carry a gun or buy any gadgets. That mind-set will create a point of reference to fall back on if your personal world explodes with violence and the stakes are life-or-death. Without that point of reference, you are lost in a whirlwind of threats and paralyzing fear that cuts you off from the ability to concentrate on what must be done by you alone at that instant to survive.

The sum of crime survival for you and your family is the same as for peace officers. The odds against you rise or fall according to your preparation and decision-making ahead of time. For all of us, the Four Rules are the heart of survival:

• REACT IMMEDIATELY
• RESIST
• CRIME SCENE #2
• NEVER, NEVER GIVE UP

No man, no woman, can be fully prepared for what may be a final life-or-death struggle. As I have talked with people who have faced this struggle, some of the same obstacles and reactions to those obstacles seem to be in many of their stories. First is the suddenness of the attack and their complete surprise that "life as usual" has turned to "life is on the line." Second is the cold reality that "I'm not being rescued. I have to do this on my own." Third, survivors are those who stand on "I will not give up—I won't quit."

Part IV

The Four Rules in Action

INTERVENING IN VIOLENT CRIMES

The death of Good Samaritans from intervening in violent crimes is fast becoming a murder statistic by itself. Still, it's possible to effectively intervene in a violent assault to help someone and not become a victim. But your intervention must be guided by three principles:

• Keep your distance.
• Keep them in sight.
• Keep the pressure on.

Oceanside, California, February 7, 1994

A man with a gun confronts his estranged wife in a parking lot as she leaves work. Two coworkers intervene verbally from a few feet; both are shot point-blank and killed. The man proceeds to kidnap his wife, take her to Mexico, and release her unharmed.

Intervening in any crime is dangerous. These are ways to aggressively help and not become a victim yourself. If you're on foot, throw something through a window, a brick, rock, shoe, anything. If you're in your car, use it—that's correct! A minor collision with a parked car or a store window to set off the alarms is a small price to maybe save a life and not risk yours. Shattered glass, collisions, honking, followed by an alarm, gets the most attention. If you think this response is too extreme, you probably shouldn't be trying to intervene.

Noise has the potential to deter a crime in progress in a public or semipublic place if it brings attention from pass-ersby who are within sight. Because of the risk of exposure, noise broadens the crook's control problem and will split his concentration. That's crucial to a victim—it distracts the crook attacking them.

At night, direct your lights at the attack. Flick them off and on and make sure you point. People will always look in the direction you point. When cops pull into an emergency call, they always look for citizens outside pointing to where the action is.

But, rarely do people call the police due to just another alarm going off. However, that alarm, along with breaking glass, a car collision, or screaming, does create pressure and control problems for the crook. Real or imagined, pressure works.

On September 19, 1994, Johnny Pagnini and a friend had

just entered a Los Angeles freeway when he saw a young woman being hit and struggling with a man in the backseat of a passing car. He said, "I chased them. I had to do it. I thought about my kids."

The facts: She had been kidnapped. The man in the backseat was trying to rape her.

The kidnappers immediately realized they were being followed. They tried to lose him. Pagnini stayed with them and kept the pressure on. They never got her to an isolated spot. After thirty miles they took an off-ramp, stopped the car long enough to throw her out, and then took off. (I hope someone like Pagnini is around if my wife or daughters are ever abducted!)

If no one gets involved beyond finding a pay phone, cops will always get there after it's all over to pick up the pieces. In my experience, intervening in crimes and cellular phones have become inseparable.

On July 25, 1995, 8:30 P.M., Keith Brown, a neighborhood watch captain, was informed of a neighborhood dispute. He walked down the street to check the address and call the police. Witnesses said Brown became involved with the neighbor in a shouting match that quickly worsened. Brown, who intended to get the address and call the police, did not keep his distance. He was shot to death on the sidewalk.

Keep your distance. Keep them in sight. Keep the pressure on—regardless of your experience.

On July 18, 1995, Antranik Geuvjehizia, Los Angeles deputy sheriff, bailiff in the O. J. Simpson murder trial, and neighbor of Judge Lance Ito, was at home about 9 P.M. He was putting out the trash when he saw a trespasser in his neighbor's yard. Off-duty, Officer Geuvjehizia chased him. He got close. The man turned and shot. Officer Geuvjehizia was killed.

More people are intervening in crimes. Not just because of more crime creeping into their neighborhoods, but because people are fed up with criminals. The three "keep" rules are, in my experience, lifesavers for Good Samaritans. Because intervention is so spontaneous, make decisions beforehand on how to help safely. You may stop a violent crime, maybe even save someone's life, and not lose yours.

Your Life for Your Property

On November 15, 1995, another man was killed, checking on a possible car prowler. The newspaper read: David Hessler, a resident of San Diego, California, left his home at 2:15 A.M. to check a noise outside and near his locked car. He was shot at close range in his front yard and died there.

I remember my first case like this one. A husband and father went outside his home around 11 P.M. to check a noise he thought to be near his expensive, parked Porsche. He confronted four juveniles. One of them, a thirteen-year-old, stabbed him in the chest. He called for his wife, the juveniles escaped, and he died in her arms.

Although slightly different from intervening in crimes against others, intervening in a crime against your property is a confrontation that needlessly takes many lives. First and foremost, never leave your home to save your property outside.

It's a tug-of-war that all men struggle with, including me: to stay inside our home and call the police while outside we can hear, perhaps even see, a thief taking our property. I recall, one late evening, sticking a gun in my back Levi's pants pocket and preparing to go outside. My wife intervened and said, "Where are you going with that gun?" I told her I heard a noise out front, near my truck. She said, "You expect so much danger that you're going outside with a gun? You know better! Please don't!" I didn't. At issue here is one of the mistakes that we men make that cause more of us to be killed at crime scenes than women. A subject already discussed in "Deadly Mistakes," but important enough to repeat. Women rarely leave the safety of their homes to confront criminals in their front or back yards. Men consistently do it because of the attitude "catch 'em, hold 'em, make 'em pay." And men die because of it.

ARMED ROBBERY OF AN OPEN BUSINESS

During an armed robbery of an open business, the criminal's objective is different from when assaulting you on the street or in your home. Whether he's robbing a bank or a small all-night market, his focus is seldom on you—it's on money and speed: get the money and get out. If you happen to be there as a customer, follow these dos and don'ts:

DO: *If you are entering* a building and realize it's being robbed, duck back out. As simple as this sounds, most people are too frozen to duck back out.

DO: *If you are already in and right next to a door* (entrance or exit), duck out if you can do it instantly. Scream and yell as you run. It will put pressure on the crooks and help the people still inside.

DO: *If you are inside, not close to a door,* and you hear, "Freeze!"—do it. Hit the floor. Obey. At this point their primary focus is the cash register—not you. If they are robbing customers, give up your property readily.

DO: *If they begin shooting or kidnapping,* react immediately—concentrate on your escape, don't be distracted by injury. There's no guarantee they'll stop shooting before they get to you. When the shooting starts, bolt and run. Don't let anything stop you—even a plate-glass window.

DON'T ever allow yourself to be tied up.

DON'T ever allow yourself to be moved, to a back room, to a meat locker, or be taken hostage.

Note: The focus here is not robbery deterrence for retail

businesses, managers/owners. Nor is it employee protection training. These are separate subjects.

Hard-Line Hostage Facts

- In the beginning, hostages have value for the hostage-takers, whether it's to get through police lines or to keep law enforcement at bay while bargaining for demands (women hostages are usually raped, also).
- At some point, be it minutes, hours, or days, hostage value ends. The hostage is in the way and a threat as a potential witness.
- At this point, if you are a hostage, you will be at crime scene #2, isolated, bound, at their mercy. They will decide whether you live or die.

At the open business, crime scene #1, you still have a chance. Scream, yell, make it as difficult as possible for them to move you. If they shoot you then and there as you resist being moved, you can expect they would shoot you later when you are no longer of value to them and in an isolated place.

CAR CRIMES

Cars are involved, in one way or another, in the bulk of all crimes in the United States. Twenty years ago carjackings, bumper crimes, car rammings, drive-by shootings, freeway sniping, chunks of concrete dropped from overpasses, were comparatively rare. The severity and frequency of car crimes has exploded.

Even more threatening to motorists is the increase in the serial killers who now look for their victims on the highways.

"One way of looking at it is to say our cities are bursting at the seams with criminals so they're moving out to the highways. We have gathered extensive information on eighty-five known serial killers who spent vast amounts of time cruising interstates looking for victims. . . . Thirty of the killers are still out there," says Louis R. Mizell, former special agent and intelligence officer with the U.S. Department of State and currently president of International Security Group of Bethesda, Maryland.

Highways are made to order for criminals looking for opportunity. Highway hunters were responsible for more than two hundred thousand crimes in the United States in one twelve-month period (mid-1992 to mid-1993). Twenty thousand of these crimes were violent and involved serious injury to murder. Criminals have quick access to an inexhaustible supply of motorists and immediate escape routes. A couple of LAPD friends of mine were involved in two highway-hunter murder series in the mid and late eighties. William Bonin stalked the freeways around Los Angeles preying on stranded motorists and hitchhikers. Dubbed the Freeway Killer, he was charged with fourteen sex-related murders and another twenty-six were pinned on him.

In the other similar highway-hunter serial killings, Randy Kraft, dubbed the Freeway Slayer, prowled the highways of California, Oregon, and Michigan. He was caught in 1988, charged with and convicted of sixteen murders, and had another twenty-one pinned on him. Both Bonin and Kraft focused their hits on disabled motorists and hitchhikers.

I call people who have had a chance encounter with a serial killer and have lived to tell about it extremely lucky. By the time a serial killer picks his target and makes his move, he has everything stacked in his favor. They're professional killers—there are few survivors.

David Allan Lucas was a serial killer. He was an opportunist who watched both the freeway and city streets. On June 8, 1984, he picked Jodie Robertson as his seventh target. The difference between Jodie and his other victims is that she lived.

Jodie Robertson's Story

I was thirty-four years old, living in Seattle, on vacation visiting my brother. I had dinner alone and left the restaurant about 11 P.M. and started back to the apartment. I was at the stoplight waiting for the light to change. I noticed a sports car pull up, turn, and slowly drive past me. He gave me a long look. I didn't think anything of it at first. Then in the parking lot, the same car pulled in. He got out of his car, but left the motor running. He walked toward me. I had a twinge of uneasiness, but I didn't feel real danger and didn't feel a need to do anything. He walked past me, instantly turned around, grabbed me, and put a knife to my throat. "You're going with me," he said. He warned me not to run or scream or he would cut my throat. I had never heard words like that. I was paralyzed, I couldn't even scream. I did everything he said and he cut me up anyway. He shoved me into his car through the driver's side, holding me so I couldn't run. He drove me to a house, walked me inside, took me into a bedroom, and tied my hands with a rope that was neatly coiled and placed on the bed. It was as if he had prepared for this. Then he moved me to another room where there was only a bed and nightstand. He laid me down on the bed and told me to stay put and not try anything. I started to cough and raised my head. That made him angry. He grabbed my throat hard and choked me until I lost consciousness for a short time.

He raped me on the bed, my hands still tied. After he raped me, he walked me back out to his car and drove me to a deserted area. It was a long drive. He knew the area, I could tell. He walked me into the bushes. He was like a machine—just do one thing and on to the next—no emotion.

I was still tied. He grabbed my hair pulling my head back, then he slashed my throat ear to ear. He never said a word. He left for a minute. I was drifting. My mind was going from one thing in my past to another. Then he came back. He had a rock. With both hands, he slammed it into my skull.

Through most of it, I was kind of in and out of consciousness. I struggled and resisted the slashing even though I don't remember it. My hands and fingers were severely cut up. The police and medical personnel say that's what saved me. It interfered enough, they said, that he didn't finish me off like he did the others. I was the only survivor of his rash of killings.

Two women out for their morning walk found me. I was lying in a semiconscious state. I heard them coming and made some noise. That was around 7 A.M. the next morning. I had lain there in the bushes since the night before. I am so lucky, especially considering that I did nothing to try to stop him from kidnapping me in the beginning. I missed several chances to escape during the ride, starting right in the parking lot when I had that uneasy feeling I pushed aside. Later at several different intersections, there were times when I could have tried something. The knife was not even in his hand when he was driving. He had placed it in front of the dash when we were in the car. He did keep one hand on me. Several times in that drive to this house I might have escaped. But, I didn't know how to try. He definitely had some type of mental control over me. I had chances but they were fleeting. I was too paralyzed with fear to even see the chances. I guess I didn't believe I had it in me to try to escape. I didn't think I could do it. I was only thinking, "What does he want, what is he going to do to me?" It never crossed my mind that I should do something. When he got me to his house and then tied me up, I didn't even resist that. After I was tied up, my chances were gone.

What Jodie Did Wrong

Everything! As Jodie has said, "I missed my chances. . . . I didn't listen to my instincts. . . . I knew it was the same car and man that had looked me over. . . . I didn't try to escape at an intersection. . . . I didn't try to crash it. . . . I was just plain lucky."

For the Record

David Allan Lucas was convicted of the murder of three women and the rape and attempted murder of Jodie Robertson. Detectives are convinced he is guilty of the murders of three additional women. He is still on death row in California and in his tenth year of legal appeals.

Most serial killers today are highway hunters—that's where they find easy prey. Your protection is limited but effective:

• Listen to your gut feelings. Be willing to think less than positive of some people under some conditions. Be willing to judge them as "not harmless" when they look you over.
• React immediately if they move toward you—explosively if they move against you.
• Hitchhiking? Don't! If you do it, you're gambling, and if they move against you, it will be in an isolated location.
• Stranded? More on this subject in a few pages—for now, accepting a ride off the freeway may be your last mistake.

Chunks of Concrete and Other Foreign Objects Hurled from Overpasses

In the four-year period 1990–94 the average number of *reported* incidences of rocks, chunks of concrete, soda bottles, etc., hurled from American freeway and highway overpasses at passing motorists was 740 per year.

Protecting yourself from this sort of random violence is nearly impossible when it's "coming down." The best you can do is minimize your risks. This is what I do:

• When I see juveniles hanging around on an overpass that I'm approaching, I start changing lanes.
• When I'm driving in a city that I'm unfamiliar with, I like to know where the gang-controlled areas are. Graffiti, on or below freeway signs, on walls or bridges, is the tip-off. Sparse graffiti is not yet gang-controlled. That translates to fewer foreign objects hurled at motorists passing through. Heavy graffiti is a sign of an area heavy with gangs and that translates to a higher incidence in *all crimes* against passing motorists.

   (Note: City workers who paint out graffiti can't keep up with it in gang areas. It's an eyesore but a danger sign and crime-avoidance tip-off for you and me.)
• When I'm in cities I'm thoroughly familiar with (San Diego, Los Angeles), I'm aware of the gang turfs and minimize my risks from overpass crimes (and freeway shootings) by never using at night the freeways that pass through those areas.

I remember this case well: He was in his Corvette. It had a sunroof. Two teenagers, one sixteen, the other thirteen—on a $1 bet—heaved a six-pound chunk of concrete. That random act of violence left a young man partially paralyzed and dependent on his parents.

I know it's either inconvenient or damn difficult to avoid all the unsafe areas on a business day trying to get from point A to point B. For your increased safety, at least do this: avoid the heavy graffiti/gang areas at night—most incidents of thrown rocks, bricks, chunks of concrete, occur, like all other car-related crimes, on interstates and freeways at night. There is no pattern to the day of the week or time of night. There are more injuries than deaths, but the injuries are usually paralysis and/or loss of sight. Most of the injuries result from the "chunk" passing through a windshield or sunroof.

Highway Shootings

Car-to-Car. The first wave of deadly roadway disputes began in 1985 in Los Angeles. As of 1993, we averaged 1,550 killed or wounded motorists nationwide per year from these disputes. Most can be avoided by a change in attitude: leave your "I'll fight for this piece of highway" attitude at home. And don't use your middle finger to communicate your displeasure with other motorists. Los Angeles gets credit for the bumper sticker:

> OK, OK, DON'T SHOOT, I'LL MOVE OVER.

Car-to-Ground. San Diego gets credit for the first city street sign regulating drive-by shootings (sidewalks, restaurants, and businesses hit by gunfire from passing cars):

© 1991 E. G. Kallen & Rick Steiner; for reprints write Box 16836, San Diego, CA 92176

The sign was placed in a particularly hard-hit gang-controlled area by a private crime-watch group. (Through it all, Americans try to keep a sense of humor.)

These are some protective measures we take to guard our family, to give us better odds:

We don't go into or pass through gang areas. This includes when we visit cities unfamiliar to us. Our tip-offs are heavy graffiti, boarded-up buildings, obviously long-term vacant lots.

We stopped shopping at those malls or going to those movie theaters frequented by gang members. Shopping malls and theater complexes that have a high percentage of shops and movies catering particularly to teens are unfortunately magnets to young gang members.

We no longer eat at our favorite barbecue restaurant or our favorite Vietnamese restaurant because they are in the inner-city gang area.

Americans hate any restrictions to our freedom to come and go anywhere we like, especially in our cars. My family's no different. But there are safe zones and unsafe zones. By necessity for our security, we no longer allow ourselves to go to a lot of places. We are fast becoming a separated society. Street gangs are one of the primary reasons.

When on foot, I walk facing traffic. I like to see what's coming, including what drivers and passengers are doing. It's a small habit from my twenty years as a cop. In my experience as a police trainer, what saved cops or got them killed were small safety habits either kept or broken.

Ground-to-Car. Shootings and objects such as chunks of concrete dropped from overpasses on our nation's highways are the clearest indicators of how random violence is undermining our basic security in America. Deborah Denno, a criminologist at Fordham Law School, said, "The growing incidence of highway crimes has overtones more

> Los Angeles is consistently the national record holder for car-to-car and car-to-ground shootings. Their worst *weekend* for drive-by shooting murders ended with thirteen dead. On August 1, 1995, a *Tuesday* night, the record became nine dead in one night. Twenty-three nights later, August 24, twenty-seven people died in car-related shootings in four nights. Most were gang-related. Los Angeles is the birth-place for America's street gangs and experiences the worst and most incidents of drive-by shootings.

ominous than other crime statistics . . . Usually, crimes are committed against people in or near the same neighbor-hood as the criminal's, but highway crimes suggest a pattern of violence against total strangers."

The worst-in-America ground-to-car random violence took place in Jacksonville, Florida, on I-295 between February 1992 and October 1992. In that eight-month span, twenty-one cars were hit by gunfire and sixteen motorists had chunks of concrete dropped on them.

Credit goes to the AAA Auto Club for their bold move in advising their members to avoid I-295 in and close to Jacksonville. Their move immediately prompted the local media to dub the roadway the Highway from Hell. That resulted in a task force of 143 National Guards-men, some using sophisticated military aircraft with night-time optical capabilities, and 22 full-time street cops and detectives.

The pressure ended the attacks, although no arrests were made. The cops I know and talked with were blunt: "We're pretty sure who did it—one of our local teenage gangs."

Since August 12, 1995, another ground-to-car shooting series has developed near the mountainous Lake Tahoe resort area on I-80 in northern California. In a seven-week span, fourteen cars were hit with bullets. Injuries, but no deaths, so far.

Protection from ground-to-car shootings, like all random violence, is the most difficult. Much like the bombing of a public building, ground-to-car shooting victims are whoever happens to be there. Your first move is to stay out of and away from gang-controlled areas.

If you or your car is hit:

DO keep driving if at all possible.

DO use your cellular phone (911) to receive directions to the closest medical aid and to alert and receive the closest police response.

DON'T zigzag in and out of lanes or go for high speed and risk becoming involved in a traffic accident.

DON'T ever stop and look for, let alone confront, the attackers.

Off-Ramp Murders/Crimes

I'm talking about not just the off-ramp but the street and lots adjacent to the off-ramp, where lost motorists wind up stopped to check their maps.

I remember a close call for my wife and me on an off-ramp street in Denver. We had landed late at night, picked up our rental car at the airport, and headed out for a speaking engagement. A half hour later, about 1 A.M., we were hopelessly lost. We took an off-ramp and pulled over on a side street to read the map. As soon as the inside light went on, I got a bad feeling. I immediately started the car and left. Then I saw them . . . three guys sitting in an idling car across the street. I hadn't seen them pull in with my nose in a map in a lit-up car.

Sometimes it's so close—the only thing between you and crime is a bad feeling. I broke one of my own do/don't rules and we almost paid for it.

I remember my first off-ramp murder. A family visiting in San Diego became lost and took the wrong off-ramp, putting themselves in an inner-city gang area. They stopped, mom driving, dad and two kids in the backseat, turned on the inside light, and got out the map. (Maps are no help if you don't know where you are.)

Two gang members walking by saw a carload of obviously lost people and wasted no time. They shoved a gun at the mother's closed window. Terrified, she rolled down the window (instead of hitting the gas). It took less than half a minute to rob them. With the husband and children watching, the triggerman shot the mom point-blank, and the robbers took off.

If the Off-Ramp You're On Is Suddenly Blocked

Unless the car blocking the road is two or three times larger than yours and you can't back up, hitting it at the front or rear corner will spin it. In most cases, your car has the power and weight to save you.

Florida and California experience the most crimes initiated via blocked off-ramps. A friend of mine handled this case:

June 20, 1991, Guadalupe Estrada, with her three young children, was suddenly blocked on the off-ramp when two men rolled a car in front of hers. From the time Guadalupe first saw the vehicle, was blocked by it, was approached by the two men, and was shot in the head—murdered in front of her children—approximately thirty seconds passed. Guadalupe was suddenly facing too many things happening at the same instant to also decide on what to do to save her life. It's crucial that you have survival decisions made before it happens.

For the Record

Both men were arrested, charged, and convicted, but of course that's too late. Both were on parole and had extensive criminal records. A survival mind-set to hit the gas could have changed everything.

DON'T take off-ramps that bear the heavy-graffiti tip-off that the area is gang-controlled.

DON'T pull into an open business that has loiterers outside or heavy graffiti.

DON'T stop on an off-ramp street or on a closed business lot at night (even if it's lit up) and bury your attention in a map.

DO drive on; look for an open business in a safe area.

DO what many safety-conscious people do. One of you consult the map, change the tire, etc., while the other watches the area. Cops do it—one writes the ticket, the other keeps a watchful eye.

You're always safer in a moving car, lost or not, than stopped in an idling car or, worse, parked and all of you lit up with your attention on something inside your car. Get the passenger to focus on the map while the driver keeps moving.

Rest-Stop Violence

Do not stop at highway rest stops at night. Some rest stops (in California and Florida particularly) are havens for opportunistic criminals. Often, they are the local bums or illegal immigrants who usually commit petty thievery. Others are the serious armed robbers and carjackers. Worse, the highway hunter will use a rest stop as an opportunity to select a motorist (usually a woman) to follow.

A woman who worked for me had, a few years earlier,

stopped at night at a rest stop on I-5 midway between San Diego and Los Angeles. After leaving and getting back on the highway, a car pulled up alongside her. The male driver honked (urgently, she said) and pointed to her left rear tire. She pulled over on the shoulder to check—he, too, pulled over . . . to "help." It's a reasonably common ruse.

He kidnapped her at gunpoint and raped her for two hours in the backseat of his car in a nearby dirt road. The rest stop where she had stopped was so hard hit by crime that for the first time in its history, the California Highway Patrol established *foot patrols* there.

Mom, Someone Followed Me . . .

In 1992, thirty-five thousand motorists were victimized after initially being observed and then followed. *Follow-home criminals* usually focus on locations they are comfortable with. Cleophus Prince found and followed most of his victims from a Family Fitness Club in San Diego from February 1990 to February 1991. Prince stalked and followed seventeen women home; he murdered six. A friend of mine had the cases.

With the exception of five, his MO was the same: Watch them work out, follow them home, then leave. Watch for them again on the same day, same hour, in the fitness club. When they showed up, he would leave, go to their home, and wait.

With few exceptions, most of his victims were attacked after they returned home and were in the shower. The knife he used to murder them with was usually a butcher knife from their kitchen. Only one victim suspected she had been followed home.

It was January 24, 1991. A young woman returned home from the fitness club. "Mom, somebody followed me home. I could feel it. He turned every time I did." Mom said, "Oh, you're just imagining things." Daughter went upstairs to shower, mother stayed downstairs watching television.

Suddenly, the mother saw a man's shadow at the window (they had venetian blinds). Someone was trying to open it. He went from window to window, trying to get in. They were all locked. She dashed into the kitchen to lock the sliding glass door. She reached out and flipped the lock a split second before Prince reached the door. She was eyeball-to-eyeball with the murderer of six women, with only glass between them.

Prince yanked at the door, then panicked, ran to his car, and got away. A few weeks later, he was arrested and is currently on death row.

Being followed is the easiest of all car crimes to protect yourself against, by following two basic steps:

First step—look around on your way to your car. Be aware of who's in the vicinity. Do they seem to "belong"? Does someone appear to be lurking? Listen to your instincts. Most people already have this awareness when they are at home. For some reason, they seem to abandon their "he looks like trouble" when they leave their neighborhood.

Second step—look in your rearview mirror. (No one is as vigilant with their rearview mirror as crooks are. Tailing them is difficult because they are experts at watching their backs.)

To increase your awareness and ability to discern if you're being followed, use this mental game some undercover cops use: three cars behind me—red car, blue pickup, white van. A block or two later, check behind you again. As you make turns and change streets, you'll notice if someone is following . . . at least you'll get a gut feeling. Initially, this takes a little concentration, but it will soon become a habit—just like being alert to who is hanging around your street at home.

When you're not sure, don't go home or anywhere you go

frequently (office, school, gym). Go to a very public place, park where lots of people are around. If he follows you, record the license number and a description of the occupants (on your cellular phone if you own one).

CARJACKING

The first wave of armed car robberies began in 1991, with Detroit cops getting credit for the term *carjacking.* In Los Angeles, the crime went from occasional in the eighties to 4,500 cases in 1991 to 7,000 cases in 1992. The crimes have also become more violent. This trend is nationwide— 28,000 cases in 1992, up 47 percent in one year.

The difference between a carjacking and a carjacking plus kidnap, rape, and maybe murder *is one second in the criminal's mind.* What he does or doesn't do is usually determined in the first few seconds by what you do or don't do.

Cathy Hartgraves's Story

December 14, 1979. I was kidnapped by two escaped convicts from New Mexico. When they needed a different getaway car, they ended up in the same shopping center with me at six-thirty in the evening.

I had done a lot of grocery shopping. The bag boy offered to help, but I declined. I wish I hadn't.

Returning to my car, I unlocked it and started to put my groceries in when a man approached me. I noticed his tattered clothing and long, straggly hair. He looked like a bum. I got that horrible feeling you just can't explain. I sensed I was in big trouble. I remember thinking, "Calm down, it's just because he looks weird." No one was immediately nearby, but there were people in the parking lot.

He asked directions to the freeway. I told him, hoping he would leave. Instead, he stalled; offered to help with my bags. I felt frightened as I started to get into my car. He acted like he was going to close the door behind me— that's when he shoved a knife up to my face and said, "Now scoot over." I tried to jump over the gearshift lever, but simultaneously, another guy came out of nowhere, opened the passenger side, and stuck a gun to my head.

They sandwiched me in. The one with the gun said, "I'll blow your fucking head off." I was terrified. I pleaded, "Take my money, take my purse, just let me go." I was hysterical. One of them said, "Calm down, we're just going to go down the road here a little bit." They constantly threatened, "Don't mess up, we'll kill you."

That began a nine-day ordeal. They kept me in the backseat—my car was a two-door. As they headed north on the interstate into Oregon, the raping began. One raped me in the backseat while the other one drove.

I almost escaped once near Portland. The one closest to me was asleep. My purse was near me on the floorboard, and gently, slowly, I put my fingers into it. My Mace spray was still there. I had forgotten about it back at the parking lot, but I wouldn't have been able to use it anyway.

I adjusted my fingers on it—got it ready—and then I let the driver have it square in the face. We were doing 65 to 70 mph. There was lots of traffic. He was screaming, swerving, skidding. When I jumped from the car, it had probably slowed to 15 to 20 mph. I wasn't hurt too badly—I sure didn't feel anything. I got up and ran. One of them jumped from the car and grabbed the back of my jacket and yanked me back. I kept struggling to run and was able to get my arms out of the jacket. Free . . . I bolted down the shoulder of the freeway. He chased me. I was screaming, waving for help. Not a single car stopped.

He caught me—grabbed me in a chokehold and dragged me back into the car. I learned later that not one passerby had even called in what they saw.

I thought, "It will now get worse for me." But it didn't. They just kept closer guard over me.

They stopped in Spokane, Washington, where they pawned my jewelry and, with the knife on me, made me withdraw my money from the ATM. Then they stayed in a motel room for the next seven days. They tied me on the bed—corner to corner—spread-eagle. It was a fleabag place—no maids ever came in.

I was never untied or alone. They raped, sodomized, and forced me to orally copulate them whenever they wanted to. When I showered or used the toilet, at least one of them stood by, inches away. At night they tied me between them.

On the ninth day, they left—just packed up and took off. I was still tied to the bed. For the first time I was not being watched. It took me slightly over an hour to get untied.

They were caught four days later in Idaho.

When I tried to escape near Portland, I almost succeeded. But that wasn't my first chance to escape. It was the first time I tried. My first chance was back in the parking lot. My biggest mistake was ignoring my initial feeling in the parking lot. He looked awful—I had a bad feeling about him. But instead of listening to my intuition, I rationalized it all away. I didn't want to offend him. When it first started—his walking toward me, pushing me into the car, even in the car and still in the parking lot—I had chances. Better chances than I had later. But I was too terrified to do anything. I couldn't think straight.

I feel very fortunate; not only because they let me live, but also because, unlike most women, I now know what's ahead when women are carjacked and kidnapped. It will never happen to me again. Because never again will I rationalize away my gut feeling.

What Cathy Did Wrong

She ignored her gut feelings when the "bum" first approached her asking questions. She didn't want to offend him. If she had listened to them, she would likely have decided to forget the groceries, his feelings, and leave. This was her first and best chance.

She should not have gotten into the car while the man was only inches away. Off-balance, she was easily shoved inside. Once in the car, sandwiched between them, but still in the busy parking lot, she could have forced him to crash it. In less than one minute, they were on the freeway and had her in the backseat bound — her best chances for escape had passed.

What Cathy Did Right

Cathy never lost her will to try to escape. She made a brave attempt on I-5 near Portland but was recaptured because not one passing motorist responded to a woman being choked and dragged. Not even a phone call.

For the Record

The two rapists/kidnappers were caught and returned to prison. One had originally been in prison for murder, the other for kidnapping. Both had extensive criminal records dating back to their teens. They're currently still in prison but on the list for parole.

Your odds of surviving a carjacking are good if you and anyone with you instantly hand over the car and all of you bolt. No questions, no arguments. Few carjackers kidnap occupants. The exceptions are women and teenage girls. Men and children are usually ripped from the vehicle, men sometimes shot. Children are generally not injured, except for minor cuts and bruises. But children are accidentally kidnapped (thirty-one in a twelve-month period of 1992 and 1993).

The two common locations for a carjack crime are intersections and public parking lots. Next are private parking lots, both residential and company.

Carjackers are usually armed with handguns and work in pairs. The most common way a carjacking begins is for two jackers to approach on foot on either side of your car when you're stopped. If you're at an intersection and first in line, hit the gas. Of course, if the light is red, you're going to have to be careful. Same thing applies in the parking lot if there's room to move and the engine's running—off you go.

Another scenario: You're at an intersection or in a parking lot, doors locked, windows up, when suddenly one or more thugs appear and smash a window. A terrifying, paralyzing moment.

They may be smash-'n'-grab crooks after your purse or briefcase, carjackers, or kidnappers. Don't wait to see. Hit the gas.

Caution: If you don't have the room in front of you, with your engine running, already in gear, you don't have time to hit the gas . . . your only choice is to bolt from the car.

In the sixties, seventies, and early to mid eighties, bumper crimes were committed almost exclusively by men trying to kidnap a woman. Less frequently, it was used to commit armed robbery (bump 'n' rob). Now, carjackings set up via bumper crime surpass both.

When approaching your parked vehicle, listen to your gut. Is something not right? (Someone hanging around, maybe slouched in a car, someone coming toward you.) You can't explain it—just a bad feeling. Don't chance it. Turn around and go back into the store or business. Contact security, ask to be accompanied to your car. Make this attitude change: street crime requires reliance on your gut,

---

In any and all robberies, make it easy for them to get your stuff and go. Some self-defense teachers advise people to give up their stuff immediately (that's correct) by scattering it all around (big mistake). This advice may have been all right for the sixties and seventies, but it's dangerous today. Most crooks are now armed and high. They have a thumbs-up, thumbs-down mentality. You take a big chance scattering your property and angering the crook instead of making it easy for him to get the stuff and go.

---

not on your intellect, and may require you to return to the store.

Danger Signals in Your Gut . . . and Worse—What to Do

Approaching your car; you see someone—something unexplained ignites a bad feeling in your gut.

You Have Several Options at This Point
- Turn around and leave, inconvenience yourself.
- Go back, get security to accompany you.
- If your gut tells you, "He's following you," hurry—it may even be time to run.

In your car (parking lot, intersection) and suddenly someone is at your window talking, gesturing, trying to get your attention.

You Have Three Options Left
- Drive away—your safety first, his feelings second.
- If your car is not running, concentrate only on starting it—do not give him your attention.
- If you cannot get your car started, if he is persistent (won't leave), honk your horn, set off your car alarm, blink your headlights.

In your car, he's opening your unlocked door, his hands are on you, you're facing his gun.

You're Down to Two Choices
- Hit the gas hard—don't worry about the car in front of you.
- Bolt from your car—lead and shout orders to your passengers.

They're in your car—you're sandwiched between them.

You Have One Chance Left
- Force a crash—crime scene #2 is ahead.

Family Carjack Plan and Drill

"What do I do if my children are with me during a carjacking attempt?" You start by telling your children what a carjacking is and that your family is going to have a plan in case it ever happens to them. Because you want them to be safe. The objective will be to escape. You want to limit his take to only your car and property.

Note: More information on how to teach children how to escape crimes is ahead in part 5.

Tell your children that parking facilities are dangerous because of traffic and criminals. Don't allow your children to play around when getting in or out of or walking to or from the car. It may be necessary for them to get in or out *very fast* to avoid a real or perceived danger.

Because the number of children, their ages, physical limitations, along with the size and model of vehicle, vary greatly, each family needs its own plan.

The best way to organize your family's plan is to take everyone out to the driveway. The goal is for everyone to get in fast and safely, even babies. Have the children work together with you, step by step deciding who helps whom getting in which door. Role play is essential for children.

Next, practice getting everyone out fast and safely; emphasize teamwork as well as speed (to minimize potential injuries from oncoming cars, practice running to the right— away from traffic).

Decide on the family move-into-action escape command. The words or phrase that alerts everyone. Keep it simple, e.g., "Emergency, get in fast" or "Emergency, get out and run."

Once you have your plan worked out that everyone understands, and a command signal that everyone knows, your family is ready for a complete drill.

Everyone gathers at the front door if you're home. The driver gets out the car-door key/remote and says, "We're going to the car, ready?" Everyone goes toward the car when you yell, "Emergency, get in fast!" Driver unlocks, everyone quickly piles in. While you are all in the car, practice your get-out-fast-and-run drill.

Parents, when preparing your family to survive violence, you must be matter-of-fact: let children know that criminals usually go for the adults first, so the children will have the best chance to escape on foot (back into the mall, theater, market, closest house) for help. If mom or dad is grabbed, yanked from the car, hit in the face—the children are to follow the family plan. Get out fast and run for help! If there is yelling, shots fired, a knife, the criminal gets in the car— get out fast and run for help!

It's crucial to your children's safety that you face this fact: you will not be able to save your children at the moment you've been attacked. If your children escape, it will be because they know how. They will have the best chance if you role-play with them your family's es- cape-and-survive drill. For many families, that little four- or five-year-old who escapes can make the difference in saving the whole family. Do not play down that crim- inals are violent and injure people—doing less fails to prepare your family to survive violence that may

---

Fundamental to a family escape plan and drill for any emergency:

Include in your planning everything pertinent to escaping. This will minimize hesitation and indecision. With children, for example, who gets in which door and sits where. The fewer decisions left to be made in a crisis, the better.

Start when your children are young; four years old is not too early. Criminals always go for the adults first. Children, especially the youngest, will have the best chance to escape in the crucial first seconds.

Having your family's move-into-action escape command firmly established in the children's minds results in their immediate switch from play to "attention." No one in your family will respond quicker to the command than your youngest.

Always prepare against the worst danger. It's an outdated self-defense type of mistake to prepare against the least dangerous first, then move up the ladder of severity until you reach the worst. It's confusing and less effective than simply planning against the worst in the beginning.

take a life. Children and their families who are prepared against the worst always have the best chance to pull through.

BUMPER CRIMES

Some traffic collisions are not accidents but criminal ruses. Bumper crimes usually begin with the intentional bumping of the rear of your vehicle or with a sideswipe. We are conditioned to get out, view the damage, exchange information, and argue in a low-key way with the other driver. You must break this habit of automatically getting out because bumper crimes are an incredibly successful ruse to lure drivers out in order to commit robbery, carjacking, or worse.

When I joined the police department in 1966, bumper crimes were fairly rare. They were used exclusively to initiate armed robbery or to kidnap women.

Now, bumper crimes are also frequently a prelude to carjacking. Typically they occur in parking lots, traffic intersections, and sometimes even while a motorist is driving. The location is usually dark, with no one around — not a geographically out-of-the-way spot but one sparsely traveled due to the hour. It will be the last thing you expect.

I remember a call at 2 A.M. for any nearby unit: "A woman kidnapped by one man" and the location. We pulled a U-turn and did twenty miles in ten minutes. We thought we had a good chance to get him. En route we learned the woman's bumper had been tapped lightly at a traffic light, and when she got out of her car to exchange information, the man hit her across the face with a tire iron and forced her into his car. Her ten-year-old son had seen it all and ran to the nearest house to make the call. We didn't get there in time. She was found later, beaten and raped.

I remember another case involving an eighteen-year-old, on her way home after dropping off her boyfriend. She was doing sixty to sixty-five in the fast lane and was bumped from behind . . . yes, at that speed. She pulled over, was beaten and robbed. I didn't say this to her, but she was lucky not to have been kidnapped and then raped, too.

If you're thinking, "If I'm hit late at night, I'm taking off," I'd agree if the vehicle that hit you is full of loudmouthed drunkards or, worse, someone threatening you. The motor vehicle laws in most countries prohibit leaving the scene of an accident without stopping, except when your personal safety is at stake. If you leave the scene of an accident without trying to exchange information, it must be because you could not do so safely. If that's your decision, drive to the first open business you find and notify the police.

If you don't feel threatened, an alternative is to keep the doors locked, windows rolled up, motor running, and wait for the other driver to approach the side of your car. Shout to him that you are afraid and want him to follow you to a safe location to exchange information. Just saying, "I'm afraid," out loud, puts you and your passengers on alert and breaks the habit we have of automatically getting out of our car to exchange information. By telling him you're frightened, you'll find out quickly what kind of person you're dealing with. Most people will understand and accommodate you. If he says, "You better get out of the car, it's your duty. I'm not following you anywhere; I want you to come back here and look at this, we'll exchange information right here"—then you know he's either a jerk or a crook.

Imagine this scene: Instead of agreeing to follow you to a nearby open business, suddenly one or more of the guys from the other car starts kicking your door, beating on the

---

When exchanging information after an accident, you're going to be nervous, fumbling, looking for something to write with, trying to remember what you should write down, and what do you write it on? Make that easy ahead of time. With your registration papers, carry a three-by-five-inch card with all the information you're legally obligated to furnish and nothing more. Never, never give any information, telephone number, or address to someone on where you live or work. Caution: Some places of employment are not even close to confidential with the information they give out over the phone about fellow employees. I have a friend who rents a post office box for this and other privacy reasons.

---

window or door with a club, or points a gun at you. Your response—hit the gas.

When you make the decision to stay in your car, stick to it. Don't weaken. Don't give in to threatening demands.

Don't let any brave soul in your car be a hero and say, "Oh, I'll go handle it for you." Would-be heroes are usually men. If he's attacked, you're faced with the dilemma of leaving him and going for help or getting out of the car to help him and jeopardizing your own safety. No matter who is in your car, insist they stay there. In your car, you be the leader, you give the orders.

When you're waiting for the other driver to come alongside your car, watch your back through the rearview mirror. Watch for a second person approaching your car from the passenger side while you're distracted. Most carjackers do not work a bumper-crime ruse alone. Rapists are the exception. If a second person approaches, it's time to hit the gas.

How do you mentally rehearse against a possible bumper crime? It may be the easiest of all mind-setting. The next time you pass a traffic accident, daytime or night, remind yourself, "If that were me, late at night, no one around, there's no way I would get out of my car or turn my motor off." Then worsen everything. Imagine the person you see at the traffic accident approaching your car door and trying to get you out. Imagine him with a gun in his hand. Then imagine hitting the gas. You're better off speeding away and being shot at than sitting paralyzed. Mind-setting ahead of time will make all the difference. Ruses only work against the people not prepared against them.

Ruses

The two most common ruses used at bumper-crime scenes to get people out of their cars are (1) asking for your help with an injured passenger, and (2) asking you to accompany them to notify the police of the accident.

Make your answer no to both. Tell them you'll go to the nearest open business, notify police, and request an ambulance.

These sorts of ruses are deeply subversive because they undermine all social connections by preying upon our best instincts—to help those who need it. It's the same with many home intrusions, which sometimes begin with a woman coming to the door asking for help ("I'm being chased") or a teenage boy asking for help because he was beaten or in an accident.

FORCED OFF THE ROAD

A car parallels yours and a passenger waves a gun, maybe even shoots at you. Or, the vehicle swerves toward you or sideswipes you. Most drivers panic, swinging to the right, losing control, and end up off the road.

Hold your lane. It's almost impossible to force another vehicle off the road, especially if similar in size, by sideswiping. Do not try to outmaneuver, outspeed, or outstop another car on a freeway or city street at high speeds. Unlike raceways, highways and city streets are not uniform. Furthermore, there are cross streets and other traffic. If the freeway has no divider barrier, drive across the median and join the traffic headed in the opposite direction.

If your car is rammed or sideswiped:

1. Get off the freeway if you know the city and can be sure you're not in a gang-controlled area. The police are more likely to be around on city streets.
2. If you don't know the city, stay on the freeway; most freeway shootings, rammings, or sideswipings occur where the freeway passes through gang-controlled areas.
3. Get to an open business as soon as possible.

If you have to stay on the freeway or, worse yet, you're in a tunnel, your greatest danger is being shot at from the other car. The best position to be in is behind the other car, although it's not likely you'll be able to accomplish this. The next best is to be in front (at least there's some steel between you and them). The worst position is to be alongside the other car. If they come up alongside you, then I alter my advice. Brake or hit the gas so they can't easily stay alongside you, but don't swerve in and out of lanes.

The other danger you face is a car crash. If you're doing 80 or 90 mph and wind up in an accident, you're likely to be just as injured as from a bullet. You're better off driving at a speed that allows you to control your car.

Clare Bundy's Story

My sister and her husband, my boyfriend, Henry, and I were in a commercial district in South Dallas, which is kind of like South Central L.A. I drive there every now and then, but I've never been scared there. I was driving my Volvo and we were about to get on the highway when we drove by a "low-rider" car at a gas station. It was really decked out—gold Daytona tires, elevated in the back. Henry looked it over and said, "Oh, cool." His dad owns a chain of auto-supply stores in this very neighborhood. He loves to "talk cars." So he started to roll down the window and motioned to them with his hand about how cool their car was.

All of a sudden we saw them lower the car, and they just tore out. The next thing we knew they were sitting at the light and were next to us. There was a sense of foreboding in our car. I thought, "Okay, okay, we'll just drive away." Damn, I knew immediately something was wrong.

The next thing I heard was a popping sound, really

loud, and I thought, "Oh my God, they've shot Henry in the head." This all happened in about three seconds, and I had to muster my courage to look over. They had chucked a beer at the car and it exploded. Henry rolled his window down and said, "Hey, man, I was just admiring your car." One of the guys screamed, "What are you looking at, motherfucker!" Henry quickly rolled the window up. I thought, "Now what?" All around was a bad neighborhood. Not a police station anywhere.

Everyone was saying, "What should we do?" Henry yelled, "Just drive, get on the highway." At this point there really wasn't much choice.

As we got on the entrance ramp, turning a curve, I saw they were behind us. All of a sudden I felt a crashing behind us and the steering was out of control. Everybody was just freaking as we got on the highway. They kept hitting us from behind. I was going fifty-five, and they kept ramming us. Every time they hit me, the steering jumped out of control. I was flipping out. "Oh my God! Oh my God!" I just kept saying it. I looked in my rearview mirror; they were flashing their brights, laughing; somebody was waving a flashlight around. It was all insane.

They could not care less if we died, and that really freaked me out that someone would have so little regard for human life. They didn't care about their car, they didn't care about their own lives. They could just as easily have gotten into a wreck.

By then, we were on a five-lane highway going over a bridge. Everyone around us saw what was going on and cleared out—either slowed way down or sped way up. No one was near us except we were approaching the back of an eighteen-wheeler. I was thinking about trying to cut over and go on this overpass to the left. I figured if I did it really quickly, they might not be able to follow me, but they were going a lot faster than I was. This all happened so fast. Then they rammed me and stayed connected to us. "Oh my God," I thought. "They're going to ram me into the eighteen-wheeler."

I swerved to the right, missed the truck, fishtailed across two or three lanes of traffic, facing the opposite way, kind of spinning. I was sure we were going over the guardrail and embankment. During that split second when the car was careening, I had the brakes on gently and I was trying not to mess with the steering wheel because that's what they always tell you to do when you have a blowout. After spinning, we ended up against the guardrail, facing the opposite direction, looking at traffic passing us by.

They kept going. When I realized I wasn't going to die, I let down and started crying. I couldn't get out of my mind, "Those guys are like walking time bombs."

What Clare Did Wrong

Nothing. The way Clare handled this could not have been much better.

What Clare Did Right

Under the circumstances, she maintained reasonable control of the car because she didn't try to outmaneuver them or outrun them. She stayed in her lane and kept her speed. As a result, she didn't collide with other vehicles nor did she flip over, as I have seen happen in similar cases.

STRANDED

You're stranded on a road or highway. Your car's broken down or is out of gas and you've already pulled the car over to the right shoulder.

This situation, while not good, is different from suddenly being attacked by a violent criminal. You don't have to react in split seconds; you have some time to consider your alternatives, to weigh the variables: the weather, who is with you, the time of day, the location, whether the road is busy or isolated, whether you have a cellular phone, is an open business near? Your first priority is safety. Your second is getting off the road as soon as possible. Most stranded motorists who become crime victims reverse these two priorities.

Your first decision: Where do you stop? Never stop in a traffic lane or in the center. Get to the right shoulder; any car problem you have on any road or highway at any time is easier dealt with on the right side of the road. The same advice holds for a blowout. In fact, you could have four simultaneous blowouts and still drive to the right. Blowouts don't affect power, they only make the ride bumpy. I'll never forget an "officer down" call that I sped into after blowing out both tires on my left. I had hit something in my haste.

Next: Never accept a ride, no matter how frantic and pressured you feel. When you're with other people, always stay together. Everyone either stays in the car, near it, or leaves it, together. Don't leave anyone behind.

Now, you have three choices:

• Leave your car to get help.
• Stay in or near your car and in sight.
• Stay near your car, out of sight.

None of these choices is 100 percent safe; it's a matter of which is less risky. You have probably heard this ubiquitous advice: "Always stay in your car, roll up the windows, and wait for the police to come and assist you." These two women relied on that advice:

In 1986—two separate incidents in the same area, about two months apart. Each woman's car had broken down on the highway late at night. The attacker used the same means in both cases.

Each woman decided to stay in the car, rolled up the windows, and waited for help to arrive. During the day on a busy freeway, this advice makes sense. Unfortunately, both women were stranded under completely different circumstances: it was night and the highway was deserted.

In both cases, a man stopped to help: *a highway hunter.* He asked each woman, "Can I help you?" Each answered, "No, help is on the way, thank you." Not true, but both felt uneasy. The hunter knew better. In both cases he returned to his car but didn't drive off. He sat and waited. Neither could do anything to help herself at this point. Neither had a cellular phone. He again got out of his car, came over, and this time smashed a window. In both cases, he dragged the woman back to his car and forced her inside. Late at night, a deserted highway, who's to see or hear their screams? He kidnapped them, took them to another area, and raped them. Each was like a bird in a cage . . . easy prey in the middle of the night.

These Are the Three Risks You Face

- *Assault*—The inside of your car is not a fortress even with the windows up and the doors locked. All a crook needs is a rock or a tool from his trunk to shatter everything. In a late-night deserted area, the odds are low that the person stopping is a Good Samaritan. Would *you* stop to inspect a car on the side of the road in the middle of the night?
- *Being rear-ended*—Even with your car on the shoulder of a highway, you are in danger of being rear-ended by a drunk, sleepy, or inattentive driver. Even wide-awake, attentive drivers sometimes drift out of their lane when distracted by something like a car on the side of the road. They even hit police cars. Every year, the California Highway Patrol loses one patrol car out of twenty to rear-end collisions.

> State highway officials who advise, "Always stay in your car; wait for law enforcement; don't ever stand or walk on the shoulder," are only partially right. Sitting in your car leaves you as vulnerable to a rear-end collision as standing on the shoulder. One study shows that inattentive, sleepy drivers are "drawn to the rear end of cars in front of them." Another recent study was conducted to determine how many highway patrolmen would be needed to cover California highways on an every-thirty-minutes basis. The results showed 33,000 officers would be needed. They have 7,500 officers.

- *Being sideswiped standing on the shoulder*—You risk the same dangers as your car when you stand on the shoulder of a highway.

All these risks increase dramatically at night. Whether you're near your car or going for help, be sure to stay out of the stream of headlights so you're less likely to be accidentally hit by a car or purposely hit by a hurled can or bottle. Pedestrians on the shoulder are as tempting a target to passing yahoos as road signs are to shooters. I've had many cases of a rock or bottle thrown from a passing car doing 65 mph. That rock or bottle becomes a missile doing 65 mph, resulting in serious injuries.

My worst case of this kind involved a jogger on the side of a highway. A bunch of yahoos (juveniles, we think; they weren't caught) obviously saw the jogger, left, and got some gasoline. They returned to douse him and obviously threw something lit at him. He burned to death.

At night, the decreased number of passing motorists makes it less likely that someone will notify the authorities on your behalf. Also, if you're on a sparsely used highway, there is less chance of your being found by state troopers or the highway patrol because their routes are determined by traffic patterns.

Leaving Your Car

The only reason to leave the vicinity of your car is if you see a specific destination where help will be available (an off-ramp, freeway call box, or open business nearby). Any walking on a road or highway must be off the shoulder and, if possible, facing traffic. Never run across the highway to accomplish this. The best place for you to walk for help is on the other side of a fence or ravine. Uncomfortable, but safer.

Stay near Your Car but in Sight

In the daytime on a busy highway, this choice makes sense. By remaining visible, you have a better chance that a passing motorist will report your situation to the authorities. By getting out of the car and moving to a safe spot nearby, you reduce your chances of being injured in a rear-end collision.

Stay near Your Car but out of Sight

Imagine a scenario where you're waiting in the darkness. A car stops and two men get out. They go to your abandoned-looking car, peer around, then quickly break in. They don't know you're a short distance away, watching them. You won't enjoy seeing your car looted, but you'll be happy you aren't in the car, caged. They'll get all your property, maybe even your car, but they won't get you.

I know that walking into the brush or trees and waiting in the darkness seems extreme, but being stranded late at night on a sparsely traveled highway leaves you extremely vulnerable. Get out of sight. Wait—maybe cold but safer.

You may have to choose between safety and comfort. The inside of your car is more comfortable but less safe. Being uncomfortable is temporary; the consequences of violent crime are permanent.

I realize it will appear as though your vehicle is abandoned and make it less likely that a Good Samaritan will stop to help. But on a lonely highway, in the dark, the chances are slim that the person who stops wants to help.

Emergency Items to Keep in Your Car

Comfortable walking shoes
Warm jacket or parka
Gloves
Water
Blanket to sit on
Umbrella (for rain or sun)
Flashlight (check batteries periodically for corrosion)
The Most Important Emergency Item to Keep in Your Car:
Cellular phone (it will cut the time you wait in the dark)

Most criminals who prey on motorists do so on well-traveled freeways and interstate highways. Most target women who are alone. Expect them to be helpful, nice, and willing to give you a ride. Most crime cases involving a stranded motorist read the same: a woman stranded, alone, anxious, cold, frustrated, and worse, overwhelmed with the feeling of having no alternative other than to accept his offer and get off the freeway.

Kristen Dale's Story

January 1985. San Diego. I left work at 6 P.M. and was on Interstate 5 when my car broke down. I remembered from my high school years: if you have car trouble, put the hood up, turn on the blinkers, and wait inside for a police officer.

I waited. It was a very cold night. I counted at least ten police cars driving by. I couldn't believe it—not one stopped. [Heads rolled at several law enforcement agencies after this case. —Author] I was worried about drunk drivers who might hit me, and also about newspaper stories about a girl in the area who had been kidnapped and murdered after her car had broken down. More police cars drove by, looked right at me, and didn't stop. I was frantic, I had waited three and a half hours on the busiest freeway in America. No one stopped to help until the man in the van.

When the van pulled up behind my car, I got scared and watched him in the rearview mirror. He was wearing a mechanic's uniform and looked like he wanted to help me. I guess that's what I wanted to see in him. I was so naive.

"Can I help you?" he asked. I asked him to call the police. He looked under the hood while I stayed in my car. "Lady, it looks like you have a problem with your alternator." I thanked him and again asked him to call the police for me. He said, "You could be here all night, lady." I thought about that. He looked like he really wanted to help me. So I got out of the car.

He showed me where the alternator was. He had me try to start the car. Still no power. The lights didn't work. The blinkers had fizzled out.

He was so cordial. I was just so sure he would help me. "Well, do you need a ride somewhere?" he asked.

I said, "All I need to do is call my husband." He said, "He's not going to be able to help you that much. Why don't you just call a tow truck?" I said, "Why don't you call one and I'll just wait." He was reluctant and said, "How will they know where you are? I'll just give you a ride to the nearest tow truck." I refused. But he kept talking. Finally, I gave in and said, "Okay, just give me a ride to the nearest pay phone."

At that moment, not yet in his van, I was scared, but I thought, "What else can I do?" I didn't think about anything except getting off the freeway. I was also thinking about the girl who was murdered. The truth is, I was not thinking clearly. I thought I had to do whatever he suggested to get beyond my problem.

When I got into the van, I immediately felt sick and nervous, but I didn't listen to my gut feelings. As we were driving away, I said, "Take this exit." He didn't do it. I said, "Okay, well then, take the next exit, please."

Suddenly, he pulled out a gun, pointed it right at me, and said, "This is a stickup."

I started shaking, fumbling—trying to get my purse. I reached for my wallet, all I had was sixteen dollars. My hands were shaking so much I could hardly hold anything. So many thoughts were racing through my head, I was totally confused. I just wanted to give him all my money and get out.

I said, "Look, just take me to the nearest twenty-four-hour teller and I'll get you money. Please don't hurt me." I kept repeating, "Please don't hurt me." I was thinking, "Should I try to jump out of the car? Should I try to knock the gun out of his hand? Should I roll down the window, scream—do something—do what?" I was panicked. I didn't know what to do.

He shouted furiously, "Get your hands in your lap, bitch. Don't be fumbling around with the door . . . lock it!" I was terrified. Was he going to rob me, take all my money, hurt me somehow, and then kill me? I was still shaking and pleading, "Please don't hurt me. Take the next exit, take the next exit, please, please." He kept driving and screamed back, "Shut up, bitch!"

All of a sudden, he pulled off the freeway onto a road

with no streetlights and pulled into a vacant lot. It was like he knew the place. He said, "Okay, now you know what I really want." I prayed, "God, please don't let him hurt me." I offered him money again. He said, "I don't want your money—that's not why we're here." He pointed his gun to the back of the van and pushed me back there. At this point, I really had no more options. He had me where he wanted me. I was crying and shaking so much I knew if I didn't calm down, he'd shoot me. I tried to act like I was okay.

He said, "Lie down. I'm not gonna hurt you." I kept pleading, "Please, please, don't." He said, "I'm not gonna kill you. You know what I'm gonna do to you." Then he raped me. He was as filthy as his van.

I kept thinking, "Is he going to kill me? Is he going to use a knife on me?" He started talking to me as if I were his girlfriend, oblivious to the fact that he had just raped me. He seemed to calm down. For the first time, I thought, "Maybe he is not going to kill me."

I was totally under his control, totally dominated by him.

He returned me to my car on the freeway and was gone. His attitude had swung from cordial to violent and back to cordial. I have heard that's the way they are. Violent people with a nice way about them.

I had made the classic mistake—worrying more about comfort than my safety. By the time we reached the vacant parking lot, I was out of chances.

What Kristen Did Wrong

Kristen knows she made virtually every mistake possible.

She stopped near the center island. Stopping there reduced her options and added to her feeling of helplessness. All disabled motorists are worse off in or near the center islands.

She made her first priority getting off the freeway, instead of safety.

She didn't listen to and follow her instincts — instead, she accepted a ride.

For the Record

The rapist was arrested and convicted. He was already on parole. Kristen marshaled her energies toward improving the plight of stranded motorists in California. She filed complaints and held news conferences that ultimately reformed policies regarding stranded motorists in three California law enforcement agencies. Furthermore, thanks to Kristen's efforts, all San Diego County freeways now have emergency call boxes within at least a mile, sometimes closer, depending on the density of traffic.

Roadway Violence Diffused with Courtesy Hand Signals?

Sounds nice, but, it's bad advice.

May 1995, LBJ Freeway in Dallas, Texas: An adult male accidentally cut off another motorist. The cut-off motorist, enraged, shot Melvin Scruggs in the face as he passed.

The *Dallas Morning News* related this incident in its Sunday edition, August 20, 1995, article "Driving Anger." Part of the article suggested that motorists consider "hand signals that can yield courtesy." I urge you as a motorist, do not resort to hand signals whether you're in or out of your car to display your courtesy (or otherwise). Especially not while driving in or near medium-sized to large cities that almost certainly have gang problems. All gangs, small or large, in America and most other countries, have and use hand signals to communicate their particular gang affiliation.

In Clare Bundy's story in the section "Forced off the Road," Clare while on I-35 in Dallas, Texas, was repeatedly rammed because an occupant in her car innocently used his hand to communicate to another driver, who misinterpreted the "sign" as that of a gang.

It's become easy to give a hand signal to another motorist, have it misinterpreted, and wind up the victim of gang violence. That's not going to change until we eradicate street gangs.

| Hand signals similar to those printed by the *Dallas Morning News* | Gang hand signals—just three of the hundred-plus in San Diego (Supplied by Officer Mark Hoffman, San Diego Police, a gang hand signal expert) |

Apology

I understand

Need assistance

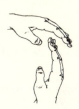

The idea behind courtesy hand signals seems reasonable. The intentions are good, but good intentions only work when you're surrounded by reasonable people who are similarly well intentioned. We're not there yet, so don't chance it.

Officer Stuart Guidry, LAPD Gang Unit—C.R.A.S.H.:

Every street gang in America, in fact, throughout North and South America, has its own hand signal. It would be impossible to give a hand sign to another motorist and not duplicate, identically or very close, a gang hand signal. Hand signals given to another motorist in or near our larger cities can be an invitation to violence. For example, here are the number of gangs and gang members in just two cities:

Los Angeles, City and County: 150,000 known gang members belong to approximately 800 different gangs.

Chicago: 120,000 minimum known gang members belong to approximately 120 different gangs.

Remember: Every gang has its own hand sign.

As high as those numbers seem, they're actually low; they don't take into account the newly emerging gangs or the new, and usually very young, inductees. And this is also worth every motorist's knowing: 75 percent of all gang members are armed at all times. When two gangs are feuding, it's 100 percent.

MURDER IN PUBLIC PLACES

If somebody walks in and starts shooting, it's not the time to hide under tables. So few people risk trying to escape because of paralyzing fear.

We train our police officers to deal with fear by channeling it into reaction decisions. Planning and decisions about how to survive a killer don't guarantee anything, except better odds than everyone around you.

—JERRY SANDERS, CHIEF OF POLICE, SAN DIEGO

As with any explosive and violent crime, a mass murder scene demands two basic abilities to give you a better chance of survival:

1. Intense concentration on escape. This enables survivors to block out everything unimportant at that instant—fear, pain, confusion—and channel their mind and body to one survival aim: *escape.* That kind of concentration begins with an attitude of willingness to take extreme risks during extreme danger.
2. Most survivors are those whose reaction time is measured in split seconds. That begins with survival decisions made ahead of time. Keep your response immediate, direct, and explosive.

At four in the afternoon on July 18, 1984, James Huberty walked into the McDonald's in San Ysidro, California, carrying three high-power semiautomatic guns. Almost immediately he began shooting people at random. Families cowered under tables, parents tried to protect their children, fear paralyzed everyone. He reloaded all three weapons two separate times and prowled the room, finishing off anyone he found still alive. He fired over 250 rounds at police and citizens until a SWAT sniper on a nearby rooftop finally took him out with one round to the 10-ring (center of the chest). He had killed twenty-one and wounded nineteen.

Never before in U.S. history had there been a mass murder of that magnitude. At that time, Jerry Sanders (my former partner and now chief of police of San Diego) was the commanding officer of SWAT and the officer in charge. In Jerry's words, "That crime scene changed me more than any I have experienced. That massacre helped me to understand more fully the value of playing out in my mind what I plan to do if the worst goes down, not only planning for when I'm on duty, but for when I'm off duty too, with my family. It's the most important step you can take to stay alive. Now I'm never mentally off duty. If the shooting ever starts, your reactions must be instantaneous and subconscious."

Whether you create a diversion, throw something through a window, or just jump through it, do it immediately and don't let anything stop you. Getting cut up going through a window is rather minor, compared to the alternative. It's a matter of priorities—getting hurt and cut up versus getting killed.

In 1991, in Killeen, Texas, another massacre, almost identical to that at McDonald's, occurred in Luby's Cafeteria: A lone, heavily armed gunman entered the restaurant. (In San Ysidro, he walked in; in Killeen, he drove his pickup truck through the windows into the main dining room.) The killer began shooting diners without warning, selecting victims at random.

My friend Al Morris and two other officers of the Killeen Police Department entered Luby's under fire and shot the frenzied gunman; twenty-three people were dead.

The one difference between the Killeen massacre and the San Ysidro one was a simple, heroic act by one man, Tommy Vaughn.

Vaughn was having lunch with friends in Luby's main dining room when the truck drove through the window and the gunman started shooting. Immediately, Vaughn picked up his table and attempted to heave it through the plate-glass window. The table bounced off—the window held. Without hesitating, he charged the window and shattered the glass with his body. Although he was badly cut, he escaped. Immediate reaction and leadership saved his life and that of those who followed him.

Vaughn overcame the paralyzing fear that enveloped everyone else in the room and survived. For all of us, the survival equalizer, the odds reducer, is not size, gender, age, or type of gun. It's our immediate reaction that counts most.

Rhonda's Story

December of 1980. I was working at Bob's Big Boy on La Cienega Boulevard in Los Angeles. It was around closing time, 3 A.M. The first thing I noticed was their dress—casual, very nice. Suddenly, they both pushed into the area behind the counter and forced the manager to stay there.

Then I noticed the gun. I was filling salt shakers at the front of the restaurant. "This is a jack," the one with the gun said. Later I learned that means a "holdup." It wasn't difficult to figure out with a gun pointed at me.

They forced all nine of us, seven staff and two customers, through the kitchen into the back of the restaurant. "Please don't hurt us," we pleaded over and over.

They were already getting violent with the cashier, hitting him a lot with the butt of the gun. I think they singled him out because he didn't understand the gunman's slang. We had to drag him with us; they hit him so hard and so often he couldn't move.

Then they herded us all into the walk-in freezer and robbed our jewelry, our tips, whatever we had. One kept saying, "We're not going to kill you. We're not going to kill you. Just do what we say." All of us were praying. We all had our own backgrounds and religions, but we all prayed out loud, together. Ditas the waitress was doing her rosary. She had the beads clutched in her hands when she was killed.

They ordered us to get to the back of the freezer. I was

shaking so badly, not from the cold, but from terror. They said, "Lie down on the floor." The cashier was already unconscious on the floor, or maybe dead from the beating. We couldn't tell and that only contributed to our panic.

We were lying on each other in the freezer. To put everything into a time perspective, only about a minute and a half, maybe two, had passed since they entered the restaurant. They sure were organized when they barged in, getting behind the registers, herding all of us into the freezer. But then they acted like they didn't know what to do next, now with us in the freezer. They stepped out and we prayed again. I've always believed at first they didn't have any intention of shooting us—that it was just a last-minute decision.

The freezer door opened. I heard the first gunshot. For an instant I remember thinking, "This isn't possible." Then I heard a moan. I remember reasoning, "They have everything, we can't do anything else for them. Why would we be shot?" So the first shot—I couldn't believe it, shooting us. No!

My hair was in an Afro and I felt the bullets pass through my hair. The first volley of shots didn't last long, probably just seconds. They left the freezer. The door shuts automatically. I remember just being frozen stiff. Nobody moved, no one talked. We were paralyzed with fear. Everything seemed to be happening in slow motion—that slow-motion feeling was weird.

They came back in. Ditas, already shot and bleeding, began to stand and said, "Oh, no, please. We won't say anything. Just leave us. Just leave. We won't say anything." They shot her again. Her body actually flew back against me. I still have nightmares of her body against me, her blood pouring onto me. But her body was my protection. Then our chef was shot in the neck, in front of my head. I remember his body vibrating against me when he died. Others were being shot, too, but they were a few inches away from me.

I have purposely not thought about this for so long—the screams, broken only with moans, dying moans. Ditas was still against me. I could feel and hear her breathing. Then she moaned a little and died quietly. I thought, "She just had a baby. Who will care for her baby?" I remember hearing the drip drip of the blood trickling down the drain in the middle of the floor. I was breathing so hard, but trying not to breathe. I was unable to control my breathing or urine. I let my body go. At that point I faked death. It was odd; in my mind my funeral passed in front of me.

Just as they left, one of them said, "Wait! She's not dead." I knew it was me they were talking about. "Let's get out of here now," the other one yelled. The door slammed.

We listened—didn't hear anything outside. Then the manager said, "Rhonda, you're alive?" "Yes!" "Rhonda, am I shot?" I moved enough so I could see him—my God, his eye was completely blown out. He kept asking, "Am I shot? Am I shot?" I told him, "No, you're not shot." I don't know why I said that, I just did. I pushed Evelyn's body off me and gave myself a once-over. The manager said, "We've got to help these people." He still didn't realize he was shot and that his eye was missing. Four people were dead. Four more wounded. I was the only one not shot.

Bryan (Rhonda's husband)

It took Rhonda years to work through this. Obviously, people are forever changed after something like that. For a long time she felt uncomfortable going into any kind of restaurant, grocery store, market, especially one with lots of people in it. Even now, we kind of case the place, especially convenience stores, gas stations. We kind of check it out before we get out of the car. We even look for escape routes, just like I've learned cops do. At first I felt a little paranoid; later it just became a habit. Rhonda's experience has definitely made us stronger.

I know a few cops and I've heard them say that it becomes an unconscious habit, planning to survive something. We never pull up and say, "Just in case this place gets robbed, you go ahead and take off." We never discuss that stuff now. We discussed it enough in the beginning that now it's just an unspoken thing between us.

Rhonda

I cared for the people I worked with. I couldn't just think of number one and the hell with anybody else. But if I hadn't known anyone, jumping through a window, going through an exit door—it would have been easier and it would have saved some lives. But the connections with friends stop you from leaving to save yourself. Without connections I could have escaped. I know that now. They had less control initially because everyone was spread out. Plus they had too many distractions. But once we were in the freezer, there was nowhere to go. Nothing we could do when they started shooting. We were at their mercy.

I've thought about this over and over in my mind. I'm positive the situation would have been different if there had been some kind of training for something like this, training beyond customer service. Maybe someone would have gotten away. Maybe that would have panicked the gunmen.

I was way off mentally. I thought, "I'll be safer if I just cooperate." Following them like sheep gave them more and more control. Those first few seconds, we had the best chances. No doubt about it in my mind.

Bryan and I have changed so much—sitting with our

backs to the walls, knowing where the exits are, looking at people when they come in, sitting in the back of a restaurant, like cops. It will give us an extra second or two. Bryan and I feel our best defense is not weapons, it's our talking and planning that will make the difference for us, give us a better chance than the people around us who probably haven't talked about it. We know if we have to run for it, Bryan has this kid and I've got that one. It's not a guarantee, but it's a better chance.

For the Record

The two men were apprehended. Both had criminal records. They were convicted for numerous crimes, including the murders in the freezer, and given life sentences. (At that time in California, the California Supreme Court would not permit death sentences to be carried out.) The two convicted murderers continue to appeal to this day.

Do What I Tell You or I Kill Her!

As Rhonda pointed out, criminals control victims by threatening their friends and colleagues. "Connections" stop everyone from concentrating on escape and taking action. I remember a serial rapist we had of over forty victims; he frequently controlled two or more at once with a knife by threatening to kill the one he was raping. The others were forced to watch, horrified and completely under his control.

At most crime scenes, people are paralyzed with fear over what will happen to them and others. Lives are lost because no one makes that first explosive move. No one shouts survival orders. I've been at the scenes and heard the laments of survivors: "If only I had . . ."

When mind-setting against crime, include scenarios and decisions that place you in a leadership role at the time of exploding violence. If it happens when your family and friends are with you, your leadership may save lives.

WHEN FRIENDS ARE WITH YOU

In a span of eleven months, starting in September 1990, a series of seven rapes were reported in a total of nine related attacks. The rapist's MO was to strike in the early-morning hours at a particularly quiet beach area in San Diego. He selected two or more victims at a time, with two exceptions.

These cases present a classic story of how easily an experienced criminal can control innocent people through threats of violence against their friends and loved ones. And, the tragic consequences of allowing him to control everyone, versus the outcome when people resist. I've elaborated on two of the nine cases.

Case #1. September 15, 1990, 2 A.M. An armed intrusion in the affluent beach community of La Jolla, California. The intruder wore a ski mask, pointed his weapon at a woman who was alone, controlled and raped her.

Case #2. June 15, 1991, early morning. A man and a woman on the beach confronted by a man with a gun wearing a ski mask. While her male companion returned to his vehicle for his wallet, as ordered, the woman was raped at gunpoint.

When men and women have not prepared against crime, the threats and stress result in their doing very out-of-character things . . . like returning to the car for a wallet.

Note: Nine months passed between the first and second cases. Though not common, this is not unheard of either. Most criminals become more active and more dangerous as their crime career progresses.

Case #3. July 4, 1991.

Barry and Kathy's Story

BARRY: Kathy and I were vacationing in San Diego. We had dinner with four friends at a nice beach restaurant, then we all decided to go down and watch the waves. About 11:30 P.M., our friends decided to go back to their rooms. It was a beautiful, warm night, so we spread our towels on the sand and fell asleep.

KATHY: All of a sudden, I felt a tap on my foot. I sat up, startled. I'll never forget it. He had a pistol, and a ski mask over his head. "I want your car keys." Those were his first words.

BARRY: I sat up immediately, too. I gave him the car keys. I said, "Take it. No problem." Then he ordered us to turn around and get on our knees. Now he was in back of us, probably three or four feet away.

KATHY: All I could think about was an incident in our hometown. These guys robbed a place and then ordered the people to turn around. They were all shot. Four or five killed, seven or so wounded, including children.

BARRY: I told Kathy, "Let's just be cool. Let's do what he says."

KATHY: With our backs to this man, all I thought of was death. I felt a sense of doom. But neither Barry nor I knew what to do, so we obeyed him. Then he handed me some duct tape and told me to tie Barry up. I was shaking so much I messed up the tape. "Why the fuck did you mess it up, bitch?" he said. "Gimme your belts." M-F this and M-F that.

BARRY: He ordered us to get our heads down. We did, still kneeling.

KATHY: Then he took my scarf to tie up Barry and move him twenty feet or so away from me.

BARRY: We had been abruptly awakened and were so completely controlled, his gun and all. I was

thinking, "Cooperate and it will all be over." I
wasn't thinking clearly. We had chances. Probably our best was when he tied me up. He had
to set the gun down to use both hands to tie
me up. But I wasn't thinking. Then, he moved
me twenty feet away from Kathy and ordered
me to lie facedown. The roar of the surf made
it difficult to hear well. Then he pulled the
shirt over my head. He had me neutralized:
tied, couldn't see, couldn't hear well, and
separated from Kathy.

KATHY: While he was taking Barry over there, I just
stayed where I was, on my knees looking
down. I was numb, just thinking about death,
praying. Then it happened. He said, "Stand up
and take your clothes off." When my clothes
were off, he made me lie down. I started to
resist, but he rammed his gun into my face. I
knew what was next.

He touched my breasts. Then he raped me.
I cried quietly. I was so terrified if I screamed,
Barry would know I was being hurt. If Barry
had known I was being hurt, he would have
exploded. I was afraid Barry would be shot.

When he finished, he gathered up his things
and our belongings, ATM cards and stuff. He
made me go a short distance with him, gun
still on me. Finally, he took off. I ran to Barry
and got him untied. We ran back from the
beach toward the houses. I felt so dirty, just
gross. Barry still didn't know.

When I told Barry, "I have to go to the
hospital, I've been raped," Barry just lost it.
He said, "I've got to find him. I've got to catch
the bastard." I told him it didn't matter. Barry

grabbed me, hugged me, and we started running up the street. We found a house with a light on.

BARRY: The guy answered and said, "What's wrong?" I told him we were robbed on the beach. I don't think it had sunk in yet, that Kathy had been raped. We have had a lot of time to think, and I've done a lot of second-guessing of myself. I was more worried about Kathy getting shot. I have had a big problem with what we did and didn't do.

We made mistakes. I guess we were two of his easier victims, we'd never had a gun pointed at us. He started off with the advantage, us asleep, him with a gun. Then he got more control over us. He tied me up, and I allowed him to do it. Separated me from Kathy. I now understand why more people carry guns, as dangerous as they can be. If something like that ever happens again to me—to us—it will end differently.

KATHY: I will never be raped again. Never!

BARRY: That beach area had a rape series going on— most beach residents knew that. As visitors, we didn't. I wish we had known, we would have avoided the area.

What Kathy and Barry Did Wrong

The rapist used their fear for each other to control them both. It prevented them from resisting and trying to escape. The only time this doesn't work for the criminal is when people have made decisions ahead of time.

What Kathy and Barry Did Right

For this young couple, what was done right was done afterward for their future. That was decision-making as a couple on what they will do, individually and as a couple, if they are ever attacked again. As Barry said, "If something like that ever happens again to me — to us — it will end differently."

Because they as a couple planned subsequent to violence, they are in a better position as parents to teach their children. I have talked to many victims who have been raped twice, robbed and beaten twice, suffered home intrusion twice, and realized in talking to them that they had made no decisions after the first time.

Case #4. July 6, 1991, early morning. A young man and woman on the beach confronted by one male attacker, wearing a ski mask and holding a gun. He tied and bound the male, then raped the woman.

Case #5. July 14, 1991, early afternoon. This was the only case where the serial rapist deviated from his usual MO. He rode his mountain bike into a woodsy state park area, then attacked and raped a woman jogger.

Case #6. July 19, 1991, early morning hours. A man and a woman on the beach confronted by a man with a gun wearing a ski mask. The male was bound, but the woman resisted and escaped. The rapist ran in the opposite direction.

Case #7. July 20, 1991, early morning. Two young females (fourteen and under) and one young male were confronted on the beach by a male with a ski mask and gun. He bound the boy, then raped both girls.

Case #8. August 10, 1991.

Dan and Licia's Story

LICIA: We had just finished watching David Letterman, poured a glass of Scotch, and went outside to sit on a blanket on the bluffs above the beach. It was a warm night, and the cloud cover made it especially dark.

DAN: Licia saw him first. A guy crouched in the shadows of the bushes about ten yards behind us, dressed all in black. He had a ski mask over his face and a gun in his right hand. We could barely see his silhouette in the shadows, but there was just enough light to reflect off the gun. I stood up, startled. I could feel my heart pounding. Still crouching, he took a couple of steps closer, holding the gun out in front of him.

His first words were, "You got any car keys on ya?" His voice was very calm, almost a whisper. I answered, "Yes," and tossed the keys in his direction. He asked where the car was and I told him. I said, "Take the car, my wallet's in there. There is money in it. Take it. Whatever you want."

LICIA: He said, "Okay, okay," but he kept looking around nervously, like he didn't really care about the car. Then he pointed to a steep path going down to the beach and said, "Okay, I just gotta make sure nobody's gonna follow me, so I want you to go down the bluff." His voice was still very calm, he didn't really seem aggressive or threatening. Looking back, I think he wanted us to believe that he was just going to steal the car and then let us go.

DAN: I knew that path was pretty steep. At that point I still believed, or wanted to believe, that he was just a car thief. I thought the best thing to do would be to follow his orders. So I said, "Okay, but that's a pretty steep trail. There's an easier way to get down to the beach, just fifty yards north of here."

That's when his tone changed. All of a sudden he got really loud and aggressive. He got up out of his crouch and said, "Shut up, do what I tell you. We're going down the motherfucking cliff. Do what I tell you!" His tone changed so fast it really scared me.

All of a sudden it clicked for me. This guy is no car thief. This is the guy I've heard about on the news. The one they call the beach rapist.

A few days before, I had read the story in the newspaper. Same vicinity, a rapist with a ski mask and a gun. Just last week he tied a man up with duct tape and a scarf, then raped his fiancée. Imagining that was really disturbing to me. When I read that, I thought of me and Licia and comments my mother had made months earlier. She had attended a crime protection program given by a police officer. She had remembered most this advice: "Never let them move you."

I decided right then, we're not going down that bluff, whatever the cost. He was not going to isolate us. It's hard to describe, but in a way that decision calmed me down.

After I made the decision not to follow his orders, I was still afraid, but I didn't care so much about the consequences. I wasn't as paralyzed with what might happen. I think it's because I was concentrating on what we had to do instead of what he was telling us to do. Somehow I knew anything would be better than going down that path into the darkness. I made up my mind, we were not going down that trail.

Nothing else mattered. It was an incredible change in me. I can feel it again just talking about it.

LICIA: I hadn't heard about the rapes in the area, so I just thought this guy was a car thief. I wanted to believe that if we did what he said, he wouldn't hurt us. When he started to get more aggressive, I felt panicky. My instinct was to just follow his orders. I started to walk in the direction he wanted us to go, but then I felt Dan put his hand on my waist and guide me in the opposite direction. He whispered one word in my ear: *"Run."*

DAN: After I told Licia to run, I took off toward the apartment building. I ran right past the guy—he was maybe five yards away from me. Then I ran up a small embankment. I thought Licia would run in the same direction, but she ran the opposite way. It worked out all right. It must have confused him.

Looking back, I think the thing that helped us most was when I stopped hoping he would just leave us alone. I wanted desperately to believe that he was just a car thief, and that he would let us go if we just did what he said. But once I realized he was the beach rapist, I knew things would get worse. To just run is pretty desperate, but it was a desperate situation.

LICIA: I think the most important thing I learned from the experience is to never let them gain control. Don't believe them. Don't believe them. He wanted to take us to another spot. Something terrible would have happened there. Thank God, Dan had read about the beach rapes and took over, told me to run.

What Dan and Licia Did Right

Everything! Dan acted on two important pieces of information he had:

1. He knew about the series of beach rapes in the area from news reports and instantly faced what he was up against.
2. His mother had told him, after attending the survival course, "Give them everything and run!"

Case #9. August 15, 1991, early morning. Two young men and their female companion were confronted by a male with a gun, flashlight, and wearing a ski mask. No doubt, he figured, easy control again. But this time he figured wrong.

He handed his flashlight to the woman as he prepared to tie up one of the males. This brave woman bolted and ran. Her reaction sparked her two companions, who resisted, fought back. One was shot in the chest, the other in the abdomen, but both continued the attack.

During the struggle to keep his gun out of the hands of the would-be victims, the rapist accidentally shot himself in the hand and fled.

The woman gave the attacker's flashlight to the police. It was a policeman's duty flashlight with a name and a badge number etched on it. The beach rapist turned out to be a San Diego police officer.

For the Record

The two men shot on August 15 recovered from their wounds. Henry Hubbard pled guilty to all charges involving kidnapping, seven rape crimes, and two attempted murders. He was sentenced to fifty-six years.

Of the eighteen people who were attacked in this series, five resisted. All five escaped.

The two brave men in Case #9, who attacked Hubbard, could have fled like the woman. That stand-and-fight quality in many men is, however, not always the only option. This issue has been explained in "Deadly Mistakes." It worked for these two men this time—it usually doesn't.

The best solution to breaking attempts to control through threats to friends and family (connections) is to talk and mind-set together before it happens.

Capt. Dan Berglund, who directed the investigation of this case, said:

"Henry Hubbard is a good example of a professional criminal. As a police officer and unfortunately a criminal, too, he was personable and likable, but it was all a veneer.

"I thought a lot about this case, especially all the men who had been tied up, controlled, and their loved ones raped. As a man, that disturbed me. I made some changes in my life. I wanted to improve my ability to protect my family and myself. As a homicide commanding officer, in fact, my whole career, I have given a lot of thought to what to do against people and how to protect myself. This case made me start thinking in terms of what we should do together against a violent criminal. Instead of talking with only partners at work—now, I talk to my family, too."

IMPERSONATING COPS

His car pulls alongside yours—you're both doing 50 to 60 mph. He flashes the badge and motions you to pull over. What usually takes place next will be part of the real police officer's crime report . . . woman driving alone, kidnapped, taken to a deserted place, raped for hours.

Louis R. Mizell, crime statistics expert, counted 25,000 crimes in the United States in 1992 made possible by crooks impersonating cops. He noted between 1,100 and 1,200 in New York City alone.

For the Record

Ninety-nine percent of cop impersonators are men, and their targets are usually women and children.

The most common situation involves a woman driving alone. The second most common is gaining entry into a private home or apartment by impersonating a cop conducting an investigation.

Law enforcement gear of all types—badges, clothing, hats, vests with POLICE on them, *Kojak*-style blue/red lights, even IDs—is available for anyone to purchase, from both law-enforcement-uniform stores and mail-order catalogs.

What to Expect

Ninety-five percent or more of impersonators will be in plain street clothes . . . at your front door or in their car while directing you to pull over.

What to Do at Home

Don't automatically open your door just because a commanding voice says, "Police. Need to talk to you."

- Detectives seldom just show up at your door to follow up on crimes. They call first. Don't open your door. Ask for name, badge number, purpose, and the phone number for you to call to verify before opening your door. Decide now that you will not be intimidated.
- Plainclothes investigators are usually accompanied by uniformed officers when in pursuit of "hot" crimes that may have just occurred in your neighborhood. If you're informed, "We need to search your home for an escapee who may be inside your home," or, "We have a search warrant, open up," uniformed officers will be there, too.

There will be far more than one or two people saying "We're cops" under these conditions.

Note: There is one exception. Sometimes federal law enforcement officers (usually FBI and/or DEA) will not inform local law enforcement of an operation and will themselves all be in plainclothes—sometimes they'll wear vests. This practice used to be common among federal agencies, but is slowly changing because it's simply dangerous for both citizens and law enforcement not to have uniformed officers present. My advice: Don't open up. Dial 911 immediately. Escape your home if men are kicking in your door (family escape plans are discussed in "The Escape-and-Survive Family Drill").

The rules in your home should be the same as those in mine: No one enters. Period! If they were to say, "We're cops—it's urgent," no change in our family's decision . . . it must be verified first. I've never met a cop who doesn't live by that rule for his own family. My bottom line: If that rule is good enough for our families, it's good enough for yours.

What to Do in a Car

- If a man or men in an unmarked car in plainclothes flash a badge, don't pull over and don't drive home. Stop at an open business. Fortunately, it's rare for police, sheriffs, or highway patrol officers to pull a motorist over while in plainclothes and driving unmarked cars.
- If you do pull over—probably due to a red/blue flashing light behind you—stay in your car. That's what real cops prefer. A cop has only two reasons for insisting you exit your vehicle: to check you for drunk driving or because you or your car match a "wanted" or "pickup." Regardless, if your gut feeling tells you, "There's something bad about this," don't get out. Roll the window down an inch (one

inch). If the occupants of the vehicle who pulled you over are in plainclothes, ask them to join you at the next open business, then leave with or without them following you. Don't be intimidated. If he is in uniform, request another officer be sent to the scene—explain your fear. Don't waver. A real cop will understand your fear.

What to Say to Your Children

• Teach your children to recognize the law enforcement uniforms common to your area. Most urban and rural areas have only two to three different law enforcement agencies. It's your first step.

• When a person in plainclothes approaches or begins a conversation with your child, the child should leave immediately. The rule is always NO GO. Most elementary schools have visits from uniformed police officers—tie your child's rules into his or her knowledge of that uniform.

• At home, with children, your family rule should not change just because someone claims to be the police—NO ENTRY, EVER.

A Motorist's Worst Nightmare

Far worse and more deadly than the man impersonating a cop is the cop who goes bad. It's only one-tenth of one percent of the problem. But, when it happens, the victim who breaks the one rule that will decrease the odds against them is beyond help.

Sam and Dorothy Knott . . . in Sam Knott's Words

Cara, our twenty-one-year-old daughter, had gone to her boyfriend's house. He was sick with the flu.

Our last call from Cara was about 8:20 P.M. She said, "I'm on my way home, Dad." She always called.

Shortly before ten o'clock, for some reason, a sense of horror came over me. Dorothy made a couple of calls to family members to alert them of our worry, then we left.

We expected to find her car on the side of the road with a flat tire or something like that. We kept stopping to call the kids back at the house: "Has she arrived home yet?" She had not.

We backtracked . . . followed the same route she would have taken home. Back and forth on each side of the freeway . . . up and down the off-ramps. Nothing.

About 5:30 A.M. that morning, my son-in-law and other daughter went by the Mercy Road off-ramp. He and Cara's sister had joined our search. They drove down it slowly for more than a half mile. At the end, they found Cara's Volkswagen.

Author's Inset: What Happened to Cara

On December 27, 1986, at close to 9 P.M., Craig Peyer, an on-duty California highway patrolman, put his red light on Cara Knott.

After the "stop," Officer Peyer, obviously using his vehicle's outside loudspeaker, directed Cara to drive on the shoulder to the Mercy Road off-ramp, then down the off-ramp and onto a dirt construction road.

No doubt, Cara must have been confused. Why did he want her so far away? What should she do? Her instincts were probably screaming out, "Wait! This isn't right. Don't go any further!"

But understandably, Cara put aside her caution. Officer Peyer was a uniformed law enforcement officer. "That's fine . . . stop here," he most probably said.

What Officer Peyer might have said to Cara when he approached her car, no one knows. Craig Peyer will not talk about that "stop" and what happened in that isolated, dark, back-country place more than a half mile from the freeway.

Officer Peyer was charged and found guilty of the first-degree murder of Cara Knott. He assaulted her, strangled her, and then pushed her body over a two-hundred-foot-high bridge nearby.

Sam Knott (continued)

We taught our children to obey police officers, and we stand behind that. It must be that way. But I now know to add this: you're not obligated to obey a command that may jeopardize your safety. Don't break hard-and-fast safety rules for anyone. Even if that command comes from a police officer as it did with Cara. If you feel you're being directed by the police to do something unusual, different from what would seem normal to you under the circumstances—stop! Do not blindly believe or obey anyone.

She obeyed him; she trusted him. Even though her intuition probably told her, "This is an unsafe place; something is wrong about this!" She was very confused; I just know it. Instead of trying to leave when she began to realize he was not "your normal officer," she waited. She probably tried to appeal to his sense of right, his sense of duty. There in the darkness, she tried to sort it all out, instead of running like hell. By the time she tried to escape, it was too late. She was isolated and under his control.

Like all criminals, Peyer first isolated his victim, then made his move. But, we know she tried. In the end, Cara won a small victory, most likely in the last moments of her life. Cara scratched and gouged at Peyer's eyes. She left scratch marks that Peyer could not conceal and that finally made him the murder suspect.

Paul Pfingst, the Prosecutor

From the beginning, this case was different in many ways. A young woman who had done everything right: always called home before she went someplace, traveled only on main thoroughfares, told people when they should expect her. When a person like that is abducted and killed, it sends a chill through everyone.

The murder of Cara Knott forced the public to face facts. Even with the best precautions, there are no guarantees. I heard this more than once during the trial: "There, but for the grace of God, go I." Particularly because Cara's killer was a cop, on duty, and in uniform.

The second issue setting this case apart from others was that women saw clearly that Cara Knott's behavior that night was identical to what they, too, would have done.

The Craig Peyer case was a motorist's worst nightmare.

To make everything worse for women in our community, we tried the case at a time when over forty women had been found in isolated portions of San Diego County, murdered. All of them nude or seminude and strangled.

As I do during most trials, I asked myself, "What have I learned about risk versus safety?" It's a habit of mine I began while prosecuting cases in New York City. Men and women in San Diego County, my family, too, learned many things from the murder of Cara Knott. Do not blindly trust people that you don't know, even those who seem okay or helpful. Yes, not even a police officer who is directing you to do something that your instincts say is unusual—out of the norm. It's a small price to pay to upset anyone, even a police officer, because you continue driving another half mile to a lighted area or a gas station instead of stopping in an isolated area. I have decided, if that upsets someone, too bad. If you're involved in a minor car accident, a fender bender, in a desolate area, and the other driver becomes upset because you insist on going to a lighted and safer area, too bad. The consequences of not minimizing your risk are too dire to do otherwise. If you're criticized for considering your family's safety above someone else's inconvenience, someone else's feelings, too bad. Most murder victims ended up in a spot where they were without any recourse or any ability to get help—a rural area, a rooftop, trapped in a private residence.

Trusting police officers is good advice 99.9 percent of the time, but not in a situation that becomes so different from the normal interaction between the police and a civilian that the "silent alarms" in your mind should be heard and listened to. Cara made the mistake of becoming isolated . . . then she didn't have any way out of it.

Facing any possible crime, you must quickly cut your losses and recognize there is not a painless or risk-free way out. Every murder, including the murder/torture case I had in New York City, began with lesser crimes, but quickly escalated and then worsened to murder.

What Cara Did Wrong

Cara's parents have said it with eloquence: "Cara's only mistake was putting aside her caution and blindly obeying against her intuition. Don't break hard-and-fast rules for anyone. If you feel you're being directed by a police officer to do something that is unusual, different from what would seem normal to you under the circumstances — stop!"

For the Record

Former highway patrolman Craig Peyer is in prison, sentenced to "life." He's eligible for parole near the year 2000. Because it occurs so rarely, it's not practical to distrust law enforcement officers. But remember, they're subject to the same psychological short circuits as all humans.

MOB VIOLENCE

More ominous than the murders committed by kids, the drive-by shootings, the violence in our workplaces, are the mobs of people who with increasing frequency attack, stomp, and bludgeon someone to death. For example, the driver of a car in a traffic accident in a neighborhood (not his own) may find nearby residents converging and becoming a shouting mob. Or it might happen to a pedestrian who happens to be of a different race from most who live in the area. This is a disturbing trend toward another level of violence in America.

July 12, 1994, Florida: A male motorist, driving through a heavily ethnic neighborhood in Miami, returning home from work (not speeding, according to witnesses, as well as a police lab report, and no alcohol in his body), struck a little girl who ran out into the street. He immediately stopped, ran to her, and tried to help. She jumped up and continued running, unhurt. But a crowd had converged. Unfortunately for this man, he was not of their ethnicity. They attacked him, they beat him. More than one shot him. They left his lifeless body in the street. Because he cared about his obligation to a little girl and the law, he stopped and it cost him his life. In my experience as a cop, I have no doubt that he knew he was taking a risk when he got out of his car. But, if he had not stopped and, instead, drove to a police station, he might have left behind a little girl needing help, and he would possibly have been charged. But he would be alive. He would be condemned for lawlessness and not caring. But he would be alive. No charges were ever filed against any of the people who beat, stomped, shot, and eventually killed him.

September 26, 1995, Indiana: Looters swarmed over four middle-aged to elderly women whose car had been struck by a hit-and-run stolen vehicle in Indianapolis. While three women lay in the car injured and the fourth dying, the looters grabbed their purses and jewelry. No arrests.

November 5, 1995, Illinois: A thirty-two-year-old male, walking through a small and heavily ethnic community, not of his race, Ford Heights, was attacked by a group of juveniles. They beat him, doused him with a flammable fluid, and lit him. He died. Two arrests made.

November 6, 1995, California: A Los Angeles City bus struck and killed a man on a motor scooter in a heavily ethnic community. Bystanders pulled the driver from the transit bus and beat him severely. At the time of this entry, November 9, the driver remains in critical condition.

The need for protection advice in how to survive a life-threatening mob is new to all of us in America. The rules we follow should be the same as those we give to our children: to never take the slightest chance, to run, to not worry about hurting someone's feelings, to not worry about what people might say later was right or wrong, to react immediately and not worry about making a mistake.

This is what I've told my family: Remember our personal safety attitude: our safety first, their feelings second. Next, stay out of the inner-city gang areas. Stay in your running and locked car if involved in a traffic accident in an area you perceive to be dangerous and a crowd forms or you just feel threatened. If you're on foot and stranded in a community or area you feel particularly threatening to you, get to an open business—even a liquor store—or take a risk lesser than staying in view on the street and look for help from the occupants of a residence. This last piece of advice is not risk-free itself, but in my experience, it's less risky.

My family's bottom line: We will risk explaining to law enforcement, even a court of law, why we may have broken a hit-and-run law, for example, or reacted in some other out-of-the-norm manner to avoid possible mob violence against one of us. Extreme danger demands extreme reaction.

Part V

Families Under Attack

You can count on criminals using the ties of family love and loyalty, and the mortal fear of injury, against you every time. "Lie down spread-eagle. Don't move or I'll kill her." "Do exactly as I say or I'll kill your kid." I have never known of a criminal attack against a family that didn't use the relationships as a means of controlling every family member.

There is something you can do right now. Parents can plan together ahead of time and then include the children (four years old and up) in their plans. This section will lead you through how to make and refine your plan through family role plays and drills . . . and what's at stake when you don't.

The first reality check in teaching your family about crime protection is that talking with children about a frightening subject is more traumatizing for the *parents*. Your children will probably love it. The process may be long and rocky, but it's critically important to the safety of your family, especially if there is a crisis and you're not there. The most difficult part is just getting started.

Bob Rogers was the commanding officer of the San Diego Police Department SWAT Team, now retired. His family's experience testifies to the critical need for the entire family to have survival decisions in place ahead of time.

Bob Rogers's Story

July 1984. My wife and I and our eighteen-year-old daughter drove to La Fonda, about fifty miles south of Tijuana and the Mexican border, for our annual family camping trip. We met with our twenty-three-year-old son, who'd been camping there for a couple of days.

There must have been about two hundred campers there. Our campsite was one hundred yards away from the others. We went to bed about nine o'clock. My daughter and son slept in the van, my wife and I in the camper.

About one o'clock in the morning, there was a knock on the camper door. "Dad, Dad!" I heard my daughter outside calling me. I opened the door and could see her, but not my son. At least four men were standing around her. It was real dark, only moonlight. I walked out, nothing on but my bathing suit—no shoes, no flashlight, no weapon.

The leader said, "You must pay cash to camp." "No," I told him, "I know the owner of the property. I've arranged to pay him tomorrow. Come back tomorrow with the owner. I'll pay him, not you. I don't know you."

Suddenly, the leader pulled out a curved, long-bladed fishing knife. I still couldn't see very well, but I checked the others for weapons. One was holding a three-foot-long piece of metal rebar by his side. The leader yelled at me, "Lay on the ground." Then, suddenly, and for the first time since this began, I saw my son. He had been ordered to lie on the ground. At times like this, it's funny the things that you notice. The leader stood at a forty-five-degree angle to me and held his knife at his hip, like a cop would hold a gun. When I noticed that, I thought, "This guy has done this before."

I had my back pinned against the camper. I refused to lie on the ground because I couldn't protect myself on the ground. I backed into an open area and started moving around, trying to keep them from getting behind me, and at the same time trying to decide what to do. They swarmed me.

The leader was still yelling, "Lay on the ground." I kept moving, staying out of their reach. Suddenly, the leader grabbed my daughter's ponytail, held her head back, and put the knife across her neck. "Lay down or I'll kill her!" he yelled.

I yelled to my son, "Lay down!" We both did, spread-eagle. I kept my head up so I could see what he was doing with my daughter. I was never so scared in my life and not sure what to do. With fellow cops at crime scenes and SWAT missions, I knew what to do. But with my family it was different—we had never talked about it.

All of a sudden the other men started kicking me and my son. Body shots, mostly to the ribs, back, and stomach. The leader yelled in Spanish, "In the head. Kick their heads." They didn't have boots on, only tennis shoes. I wasn't worried or even thinking about the kicks. I was focused on one thing: the guy with the knife on my daughter. What was going to be his next move?

Suddenly my wife rushed out of the camper and saw my son and me on the ground. They yelled to her, "Lay on the ground." She wouldn't.

It was getting worse—fast! I was shocked by the speed and how everything was getting beyond my control. I had never been in a situation where I didn't have control.

When I had first stepped out of our camper, maybe forty seconds earlier, I wasn't worried. Even as it began to escalate, I thought, "I can handle this." Big mistake.

With a golf swing, the guy with the rebar hit me above the eye. Everything went fuzzy. I remember thinking, "Uh-oh, that was bad, a hard hit." My eye closed immediately. I feared I wasn't going to be able to work against these thugs to save my daughter, my family. Everything was happening so fast—too fast to think about what to do next. I was just reacting.

The next thing I remember was a guy coming toward me with a rope to tie me up. My wife was screaming, "You can't do this. Leave us alone. Take our money. Let us go." She was getting real mad.

I was still coming back from the blow to my head; things were still fuzzy.

Then the one with the knife on my daughter started unbuckling his belt. When Terry saw that, she attacked.

These memories are vivid—too vivid—they're tough. The leader stabbed Terry again and again. Terry stayed on her feet—hurt badly, but mad as hell. She told me the anger kept her going. She was yelling, screaming, coming on strong. She has said, "I thought it was up to me to save my family." She wouldn't lie on the ground, she wouldn't do anything they ordered her to do.

The fuzziness was leaving me. I let out a half-scream, half-growl. Someone once told me to do that. I had never screamed before. Now, I wasn't going to stop until I stopped them. The half-screaming, half-growling, and hating them made a lot of difference for me—it carried me.

I leaped from the ground and got between Terry and the guy stabbing her. We were at a cliff—maybe a forty-foot drop. I grabbed him, spun toward the cliff, tried to throw him off. We fell into a fire pit of hot coals just short of the cliff's edge. We were both getting burned, but I was on top.

I needed his weapon to fight the others or my family was finished. I figured they would attack me from behind any second. I was afraid of being taken out with that metal rebar again. I punched him over and over while fighting him for the knife. He stabbed back. He got me more than once, but I didn't feel anything. I grabbed for the knife, got the blade. A death grip. He yanked it back from my grip. I was cut badly, the muscles and tendons in my hands were sliced through. I grabbed furiously at the blade again and again. But each time I got a grip on it, he yanked it back—slicing me more. Suddenly, I got it from him. I stabbed at him. But my hands were so badly sliced that I had almost no grip. So many years ago, and it's as clear as yesterday.

The knife kept slipping out of my hands. I was frantic, still screaming. "Any second they'll hit me from behind, blindside me again"—that thought kept rushing through my mind. Suddenly, the knife blade was plunged into his eye. I really don't know whether it was my force or his to get control of the knife that resulted in that final thrust. The only conscious thought I remember from that instant was, "Now I have a chance to stop them."

He was motionless. I jumped up, spun around to fight someone else. I was practically crazy with fear and anger. It helped me, it drove me.

Suddenly, I realized my daughter was next to me. In that screaming melee, she had rushed to help me; she was fighting him alongside of me. She had broken free when her mother attacked them.

With their leader out of it, the rest of the thugs took off.

I checked my family. Daughter, okay. Son, okay. He had rushed one of the four who was holding a boulder and getting ready to smash his head. My son later told me that my screaming and growling got him going. He grabbed one of them and they rolled down into a deep gully, fighting. When I checked Terry, I almost went into shock. I felt sick. She had five stab wounds, hip and chest. She was soaked in her blood, but alive. I don't pray much, but I did then.

I yelled out, "We're going for the border." We took our camper and van, left everything else, and headed north.

I was covered in blood, too, bleeding from stab wounds I didn't even know I had. Terry was much worse off.

It took us maybe forty minutes to get to the border—the longest forty minutes of my life, not knowing if Terry would make it.

I flew through the tolls nearing the border. But the mass of cars lined up at the border checkpoint stopped me. I jumped out, abandoned my car, grabbed Terry in my arms, and ran across the border, screaming for help. The police and customs officials grabbed us and took over.

Everything in our family has changed . . . for the better. Terry made it.

Before that night, I thought I was the protector of my family. I always thought, "I'm a cop. If I'm with them, there's no need to worry." But when I stood there, only feet from the man with a knife on my daughter's neck, I felt powerless. I almost lost my wife and daughter.

I really work hard at not thinking about what happened that night. Still, I have changed plenty, especially my habits, to better protect my family. The first thing is not to isolate yourself. If there had been other campers near, this would not have happened. We were isolated, easy victims. We were only a hundred yards away from other campers, but they couldn't hear our screams over the sound of the crashing surf.

It happened so fast I had no time to plan or to think of any alternative in those first few seconds.

That night, for the first time in my life, I was truly scared. I had no plan of action because I had not included my family in any of my decisions. I've camped with fellow police officers many times. As cops, we always talked and planned, asked each other a bunch of what-if questions. But I didn't talk with my family.

As bad as it was, it could have been worse. What if they had had guns? If they had successfully tied me up? If my wife and daughter had not fought back? We survived because we all fought back. And Terry, she made the difference, she was the leader that night.

I know this from experience: the toughest part of any crisis is the decision-making when everything is going down.

It was pure luck they didn't finish me while I was on the ground. I thought obeying them was best and my only option. But in reality, doing what they ordered was the worst thing for me and my family. Obeying them worked only for them, made me an easier target. And they almost took me out.

Terry has said, "I felt it was over—my daughter was going to be raped, my husband on the ground, almost dead. Something in me just exploded. I felt I was fighting for all of us."

If Terry had not attacked the leader with the knife, I don't know what would have happened to us. Our family exploded when my wife took them on. We turned on them like madmen. No doubt in my mind, that made the difference. Together, we were more than they could control.

What the Rogerses Did Wrong versus Right . . . Bob Said It Best

We were isolated from other campers. . . . I considered myself the protector of my family and never made survival plans with them. . . . Terry's explosiveness snapped our family out of frozen fear and sparked us to a furious fight-till-we-win determination. . . . I owe so much to her.

For the Record
The three remaining suspects were apprehended, charged, and dealt with by the Mexican authorities.

HOME INTRUDERS

Home intruders are the worst of criminals. Period. Their crimes include rape, severe beatings, sometimes torture and murder. It's bad, whether you're a citizen or a cop, because your home now has all the characteristics of crime scene #2. Isolation, time, control by the attackers—all come together in a place your family considers familiar and safe. As Bob Rogers, Rhonda, and the Carlson family (next story) found, their fears for their family, their friends, their coworkers, froze them up. The attackers used the victims' emotional bonds to terrorize them and control their actions.

Burglars want only your property and will wait until the homeowner leaves. Intruders are terrorists without a political agenda—they *want* to confront you, control you, injure you. Home intrusions result in the highest rate of serious injuries and murders of all crimes: 35 percent of victims are seriously injured or killed, a far higher percentage than with armed robberies, which result in a 10 percent murder rate (percentages of serious injuries during armed robberies not available). Franklin Zimring, a professor at the University of California, found in his research of murders during home intrusions that residents are six times more likely to be killed during an armed intrusion than a street mugging and robbery.

Note: Louis Mizell, security and data consultant (quoted earlier), reviewed all home-intrusion cases nationwide in 1991. He found there had been 480,000 home intrusions with 144,000 occupants seriously injured, raped, or killed.

As with reports on other violent crimes, home-intruder cases tend to all sound alike. I remember this one case that upset every cop on the department. A family was terrorized by four hoodlums for three hours in their beach cottage. The father was beaten and tied up; both mother and daughter were raped, sodomized, and foreign objects (rat-tail comb, champagne bottle) used repeatedly on them, with son and father forced to watch. Finally, after three hours of savagery, they robbed them. They left behind a ransacked home, a savagely beaten and violated mother and daughter, a shattered family.

No one knows why armed intruders are so brutal, sadistic. Criminal psychologists venture opinions, but all we really have are educated guesses. But case after case, all

---

The two ways home intruders get in:

1. Crash in — burst in (the most common).
2. Ruses— looking for someone, solicitors, etc.

In some large police jurisdictions, they average one a day — Los Angeles, for example.
   Three ways to protect your family:

1. Family escape plan (the most effective by far).
2. Locks, lighting, alarms, dogs.
3. Guns (the most ineffective by far— in part 6, I explain why in detail and lay out the solutions).

---

crime investigators learn criminal behavior patterns, not why but what happens. When a woman is abducted by a gang, a cop knows it is destined to be long and horrible. When home intruders break in, if the family is at home and trapped inside, a cop knows it is going to be long and horrible. If you're ever faced with an intruder, he will be a career criminal—I've never known of an "intrusion" when that wasn't true. Property loss will be nothing compared to the crimes against people, especially women and children. With isolation and control, the crimes escalate from robbery to terrorism and sadism almost every time.

Home intrusion is one of the few scenarios where mental preparedness and immediate response to attack are insufficient, where mind-setting must be supported by role play, a family drill. The best chance you have to escape and survive is to have a plan that every member of your family (over four years old) understands and has practiced.

It's hard enough for one person to escape violence. It's practically impossible for a family to escape when they have no mutually understood objective. You can't make decisions in the split seconds you have available because no one even knows what you should be trying to do. You have no resources to fall back on. However, if the worst strikes, families that have mind-setted together to escape and survive have a chance.

Frank Falzone's Story

Inspector Falzone, San Francisco Police Department, recounts his worst case:

San Francisco, April 19, 1974. Annette Carlson and her husband, Frank, a couple in their twenties. It was a Friday, about midnight. A male suspect invaded the old Victorian home they had painstakingly renovated. It was an extremely beautiful house in a middle-class neighborhood near San Francisco General Hospital, not a high-crime area. The suspect gained entry by climbing into the upstairs bedroom area. Annette had just gone to bed. Frank was still downstairs with work he had brought home. Startled, Annette screamed. Frank ran upstairs. The suspect had a knife. He told them they wouldn't be harmed. "I only want money," he said. Holding the knife on Annette, he ordered both of them downstairs into the living room. The knife on Annette controlled them both.

Frank Carlson tried to reason with the intruder. He kept pleading, "Please, please, we'll give you anything you want. Just don't hurt us." The suspect then cut the electrical cords off various lamps in the living-room and front-room area, then used the cords to tie Frank to one of the dining-room chairs. The Carlsons still did not resist or try to escape in any way. Threatened and controlled by the knife, they were paralyzed with fear.

The intruder demanded money again. Annette was sent upstairs to get the money. The suspect guarded Frank with the knife. Sadly, this case is typical of how easily intruders control people, even send them to other parts of the home to get money, rope, whatever, while one family member is guarded.

Annette returned with a jar containing about six dollars in coins. The suspect was livid. "You don't call this money! This is ridiculous! I want money!" Swearing angrily, he asked Annette, "Do you have a hammer?" She answered yes. Another typical and sad part of this case and many similar to it—few citizens understand the viciousness of criminals. Newspaper and TV news stories seldom detail all the crimes committed. Any experienced cop would have known there's only one reason he wanted a hammer. She went into the kitchen and returned with a hammer. He again demanded money. She said, "This is all the money we have right now. We can write you a check." Suddenly the suspect began beating

Frank in the head with the hammer. Tied to the chair, he could not protect himself. The escalation of violence against isolated or bound innocent victims is always sudden.

It was a carpenter's hammer with a wooden handle. He actually broke the head of the hammer off the handle, he hit Frank's skull with such force. As is often the case, the intruder went into a killing frenzy. He then picked up a potted plant and smashed it into Frank's head. I'm talking about a potted plant with a circumference of about eighteen inches, big and heavy. Then the suspect grabbed a three-inch-thick cutting board and began smashing Frank's head again. He swung so hard a corner of the board broke off. As is so often in cases involving armed intruders, Annette was forced to witness her husband's murder.

Annette was screaming but she felt that nothing was coming out anymore. Probably didn't matter, the suspect had turned the stereo way up. Annette was horrified, but even worse, she was paralyzed. The suspect then grabbed the thick glass jar filled with coins and smashed it over Frank's head. By that time Frank was dead. During the trial, the coroner of San Francisco testified that he had never seen a human skull so destroyed.

The suspect then forced Annette upstairs. His words were, "When I'm high on coke, I can fuck for hours." Annette pleaded, "Please don't kill me." Then the raping began. Oral, anal, everything, without stopping. He did everything. He raped her for three hours. Annette pleaded, "Please, just let me live." He laughed and looked straight at her and said, "I can't let you live, you know who I am. I have to kill you."

Three hours of rape—finally he was through with that second phase of crimes. Then he began another killing frenzy. He picked up a small rocking chair, Annette's childhood chair, and began beating her with it, fracturing her jaw, dislocating her shoulder, and ripping open her head. The rocking chair was crushed into many pieces. He then picked up a towel from the bathroom and wrapped it around a paperweight rock from her dresser. With tremendous force, he swung that makeshift weapon at her head over and over. Every time he hit her, flesh ripped from her head.

Annette rolled onto the floor, bleeding profusely. "Please just let me die, don't hit me again, please don't hit me again. Just let me die," she begged. Every time she pleaded, he laughed. He then sliced her wrists with his knife, left her, and went downstairs.

I know I'm being graphic. I'm relating this case as it happened—without any sugarcoating. If reading this helps some families prepare against our worst criminals, and there are no worse than armed intruders, maybe some good will finally come out of this case.

Because the Carlsons had been remodeling their home, they had paint thinner and kerosene around. The killer doused Frank's body, then he went upstairs and doused Annette with the flammable liquid before dropping matches upstairs and downstairs. Then he fled.

Annette, bloodied and broken, miraculously crawled out the same window the suspect used to enter the house. From the rooftop, she screamed for help. Neighbors heard and saved her.

Big-city homicide investigators are seasoned, but we were stunned at what we saw. The house was almost destroyed upstairs but the fire had extinguished itself downstairs.

When I got to the hospital, the doctors had shaved Annette's hair off. Her head was like a large orange with big chunks of skin missing. The doctor looked upset and angry when he said to me, "I'm going to let you into the operating room because we don't expect her to live. So, while we're operating, we're going to let you try and talk to her. I hope you can catch the bastard." They scrubbed me up, dressed me in surgical greens, and let me in with the surgical team to talk to Annette. The whole time this brave woman believed she was dying and knew her husband was dead and still did her best to talk to me. I was a police officer and homicide detective for twenty-eight years. In all these years, I've never been more proud to be a cop and part of a team trying to bring a monster to justice.

Annette gave a near perfect description of the suspect. For five weeks I visited her at the hospital trying to find out what we might have missed, what we could do that we weren't doing. Her father was a design engineer and an artist. He wanted to help. I said, "The jewelry that was taken, if you could draw what those pieces look like, I'll put out a wanted bulletin and see if we can't come up with a break in this case." Many of the stolen items were antiques, mostly family heirlooms. He drew some perfect pictures.

A month or two later when we figured the pieces would be hitting the pawn shops and jewelry stores, I went to friends at the *Chronicle* and Channel 7. I asked them to please put out a public plea for anybody that might have seen these pieces of jewelry. They jumped on it—in less than twenty-four hours I got a phone call from a jewelry designer who had just come across a ring that matched our description. I ran down to the store, got the ring, and headed to the hospital. I remember this day like yesterday. There are good days and bad days being a career cop—this was one of the good ones.

Annette took one look at the ring and started crying. It had been her grandmother's. The nurses were crying, and I have to be honest with you, I got a big lump in my throat, too. That ring broke the case. We backtracked that ring two times and finally came up with the suspect.

What the Carlsons Did Wrong

Sadly, as with most couples, no survival decisions were made ahead of time. They were not prepared for the privacy of their home to become a place of terror and isolation. Instead, the attacker used their ties of family love and loyalty against them. It always happens. He was able to cut cords off lamps, tie Frank up, and send Annette to other rooms to get things. Through fear he controlled them completely even though they were sometimes in separate rooms.

For the Record

The intruder was sentenced to death, but in 1978, the California Supreme Court reversed all death penalties. Chief Justice Rose Bird made a public statement that she did not believe in putting any criminal to death. In Frank Falzone's words, "While a prisoner, he has married and fathered two children, something he deprived Annette and Frank of. Now he comes up for parole every two years. It's a crime what families go through."

When the trial is over, the criminals are dealt with, the cops, lawyers, judge, and jury go home. It's all over for them, but it's never over for the victims or their families. They get life sentences.

One question I'm often asked is, "What should I do if an armed intruder is holding my wife and has a knife to her throat or a knife or gun to my child's head?"

My answer begins, "This is the first thing he'll say: 'Do exactly as I say or I'll kill her . . . I'll blow this kid's head off.'" Folks, it never changes. They control us with the same MO; it worked against others, they'll try it against us, too.

While holding one family member under threat of death,

they frequently order other family members to go and get rope, tape, etc. Like Annette Carlson, terrified family members obey out of fear for loved ones. This results in tied-up family members and escalates to complete control. Also, male family members (teenage boys and older) are always ordered to the corner of the room, or a windowless bathroom or closet, far away from the intruder, due to his apprehension of being attacked by a good-sized adult male. Home intruders always first seek to control adults, especially men, and it's during these efforts and the first few seconds that children have the best chance to escape.

Don't help the intruders. If you go get rope and or help tie up family members, you are actually increasing the potential for violence later because you are helping them control everyone and minimizing individual family members' chances to escape.

If you obey the command to get to the other side of the room, lie down near a corner, allow them to lock you in another room, once again you don't deter violence but contribute to the criminal's control. You're reducing his problem and making it easy for him.

What to Do When Your Wife/Child Is Held at Weapon's Point. Get within arm's reach of the intruder holding your loved one. Take a no-retreat position. Get close, look him in the eye, and place your hands on your wife or child, ready to take her back.

Spit these words in his face in a deep, mean, hate-filled voice: "You can have everything I own in the house, the car, I'll tell you how to get into the safe. . . . But if you touch this woman (my little girl), I have nothing left to lose. You can shoot me, stab me, but I'm close enough to get you and I will. I've killed before, I'd do it again." I don't care if you've never killed a man. I don't care if you've never been in any form of mortal combat. I don't care if you're stretching the facts. Say it and mean it, so he believes it. Use every street or gutter word you know. As a young cop, I used to practice what I planned to say to crooks at a "hot" crime scene—I wanted it to come right and real believable. When your or your family's life may be at stake, you need to do the same. Your objective is to make him feel, from close range, that he's up against as much of a son-of-a-bitch killing bastard as he is himself.

Say it, mean it, ready your body, set your mind. The crucial seconds of the scene I've pictured for you will fully define you . . . what you stand for and against. I've been at the scenes, talked for long hours with the families. The worst of the worst are intruders. Replay one of the scenes for yourself—go back to the Rogers family story and read again how Bob's mind and eyes saw it, how his body and hands felt it.

Your objective at this life-threatening juncture is for him to feel fear. No criminal will feel fear until you're inches from him. He won't feel fear if your family is all tied up, separated into other rooms, with you across the room, not even within arm's reach. Believe me, he doesn't fear the consequences of being caught and criminal justice.

Remember, the option to him "You can have everything" is as important as your within-arm's-reach threat to him.

People ask me, "Is an intruder, the worst of the worst, really going to feel fear by my saying I'll try to kill him if he doesn't take just my property and leave my loved ones alone?" If he's a psychopathic killer, the likelihood of your instilling fear in his spine is small, and he may in fact use the weapon against your child. But now ask yourself, if the worst happens, would you rather be next to him in arm's reach or tied up in a closet?

Your only chance to intervene and perhaps save what's left of your family is to be very near the killer. Family members who are tied up, separated, completely controlled, have no recourse when the intruders' crimes are finally through, after torturous hours, and they decide to kill and leave no witnesses.

In the most extreme of situations of armed-intrusion terrorism, remember that your objective is to escape. At least get one family member out who can go for help. As dangerous as all these examples and directives sound, your only alternative is to do nothing and allow them to tie you all up, separate you, and then decide how they'll end it for you. If you think about it, a "plain old" house burglar crosses a heavy law and social line when he sneaks into a private home. How many more lines does an intruder cross when he bursts into an occupied home? Are there any crimes he will not commit?

TEACHING FAMILY SURVIVAL

If your one sure place of security is breached by intruders, it will be far less dangerous if you have planned and practiced your escape. Do not stay and defend it. When you plan and role-play with your children, make certain everyone understands that your family escape plan is against fire and intruders. Two life-threatening crises, one escape plan.

Whether your family has two members or ten, they should scream, yell, shatter windows. If you have a dog, all the better—he'll go crazy (always a signal to cops). It should sound like chaos. But it is planned chaos, with one family objective: *escape.* (Waiting in bed pretending to be asleep is wishful thinking—believing that crimes don't get worse and intruders will go away if we just close our eyes.)

Crash through a window if necessary. To minimize cuts, go through at full speed. I once chased a man in a darkened house and didn't know a sliding glass door was in the way. I ran through it full bore and got three minor cuts. If there is no other exit from a fire-ravaged house or an intruder stabbing you, you have a choice: stay or burst through a window. Even if you're on the second floor, you're better off breaking a few bones than staying where you are.

I remember a case: the call was a frantic woman's voice. "My ex forced his way in. He's got a knife. He's going crazy." When we got there, a neighbor, bleeding from a stab wound, met us. He had tried to intervene and help her. We got to the second-level apartments about the time a window shattered overhead. Out crawled a bleeding woman, who dropped. She hit a wooden fence and broke a few ribs, but she was alive. She had been stabbed twice before she made it out the window.

Family escape drills are not intended to permeate your daily lives with fear and paranoia. They simply give you survival decisions to fall back on when a life-or-death emergency explodes into your life. Drills are essential because the danger is multiplied by your fear for your loved ones. You must discuss in advance the need to escape and how. Husbands and wives should be prepared to separate from each other to help the children. In practice, no man can bring himself to leave his wife in the house, but wives should leave their husbands, especially when children are involved and need help escaping.

The reason: Few men are raped and tortured with family members forced to watch. But with women and teenage girls, the severity and length of time, involving rape and other sex crimes, greatly increase. The likelihood of leaving no witnesses behind also increases.

A question I'm often asked is, "Should one of us leave our children if it will speed up our getting help and breaking their control?" My answer is, "In theory it may sound logical because intruders are seldom after children, but in practice I've never met a parent who would leave their child."

The objective is for someone to escape and get help. It takes only one person—the most likely to succeed is a child—running to a neighbor. There's a big difference between the police showing up ten to fifteen minutes after someone goes for help and spending three hours controlled and at the mercy of psychopaths.

With adults, the mental conditioning alone—visualization, decision-making—has proven to work exceedingly well. Children, however, need a drill to accompany mind-setting because they don't yet have the life experiences to draw on to accurately imagine the crucial steps to escape. Actual practice, including suggestions from them, hands-on participation, and role playing, are essential. Not only will the children know what to do in an emergency, they will gain confidence as good decision-makers when afraid.

Your goal is to train the children to respond immediately toward *escape*. The information, skills, and rationales do not change from age group to age group.

TEACHING CHILDREN CRIME ESCAPE

You can start teaching crime escape at an early age—four or five years old. Always begin with the most serious scenarios—armed intruder, abduction on the street. Escaping the most serious situations is the easiest to teach because the safety issues are obvious. Hard-and-fast rules leave less room for misinterpretation. Also, ask yourself, is our plan as simple as possible?

Use the word *intruder*. (I prefer *intruder* to *invader* because TV and movies frequently attach other meanings to *invader*.) Because children fear the unknown, defining *intruder* and using that word will help them identify and know when they are in danger from that kind of person. This will help them respond more quickly.

Be specific. Advice like "Be careful" doesn't help; vague directions are confusing. Use the word *escape*, not *run* or *get away,* for the same reason you use *intruder.* It means one thing only.

Foster Cline, psychiatrist, author, explains how to discuss serious subjects with children without terrifying them:

When parents can talk to their children about bad situations matter-of-factly, it inoculates the kid against being as traumatized by it. Whether it's divorce, death in the family, or a friend of the family being killed, kids always handle tough situations as well as their parents handle it. That's the key. Kids handle crisis, current or future, in the same manner their parents deal with it. This issue was studied in World War II when it was discovered that the main variable in how children handled the air raids in England was determined by the bomb shelter warden and parents, not by how close the bombs fell. When the shelter warden or parents were panicky, those emotions emanated directly into the children and they, too, became panicky. But when the shelter wardens and parents said things like "Dumb Germans, bombing up there, while we're down here" and led everyone in "God Save the Queen," the kids responded with optimism and strength. No one minimized the danger during the air raids, they just handled it well. . . .

When parents deal matter-of-factly with danger themselves and do the same with their children, the results are stronger and safer children. I see many overly protective parents and hear from them, "We don't wish to needlessly worry our children by discussing traumatizing subjects with them." My answer is simple: The person you are worrying over is you, and you can be certain your worry is going to rub off onto your children. Kids are quick to pick up on parental feelings. So, the secret to preparing children is to discuss the danger in matter-of-fact terms. Use adult language, never sugarcoat the danger, be clear in defining the danger—if the danger is home intruder or kidnapper, use those words, not *bad people, thieves,* or *burglars.* Don't leave any "dangers" undiscussed.

Most children will quickly figure out that some of the subject is being skipped and ask you or, worse, ask someone else. That someone else may give them bad information. I believe in being so matter-of-fact with kids that I recommend parents say, for example, "Richard, some people, only a few, are so dangerous they would shoot you and you might not live through it, and this is what we're going to do to protect ourselves just in case—so we'll be safer." When parents cope well, their children follow that lead and cope just as well.

Use television as a tool for learning (it's possible). Television generally teaches children that criminals can be tricked and outwitted. This may be great entertainment, but it hardly reflects reality. Your children need to know this.

Mentally prepare your children with decisions made ahead of time about how to respond to an emergency, using news stories and the three steps in "Mind-setting against Violence." Repeat them when watching a crime or fire scene on television. Do the unforgivable and interrupt the show. Ask, "If that happened to us, what would we do? What's our family plan?" Essentially, you are doing the same thing for your family that I've already instructed you to do for yourself.

And, yes, "Expect to be injured" applies here. Children, too, need to be prepared to overcome the paralyzing effects of fear of injury.

Expect the question "Will I be shot, Mom?" Answer directly, honestly, and matter-of-factly, but be brief. It will probably come up again. Every time, deal with it. This way you won't bog your children down with worry. Use positive responses directed at overcoming fear, so that the children are oriented toward escape, not worry. For example, say, "Even when you're really afraid, even if you get hurt, even if you think you hear a gun, brave people like us do hard things." Don't focus on severe injury. Focus on escape. You will plant the seed that injury may happen, but it will not stop them because they have an important job to do. If this seems too grown-up, too heavy for kids, look at it this way:

to prepare children against the worst, you must include the worst they may face. Children must have some advantage in case they face a life-or-death emergency and they're alone.

Parents, you have two choices: (1) Give your children the facts: children and teenagers are sometimes shot at or are in the line of fire, and here's how they can save themselves if it happens. (2) Or leave their survival to hope and luck. I find in my children and teen programs they are eager for this information.

Do not make protection a game. I'm not saying to make it so grim everyone is afraid to smile or laugh, but don't call it fun or a game or treat it lightly because the children will treat it lightly, too. When practicing your escape drill, the entire family must be present—no exceptions. When given important jobs or roles, young children take it very seriously. (Ask any kindergarten teacher.)

The warning "crime scene #2" should also be used with children. Neither you nor your children will ever forget those words. Adults have little chance to escape at crime scene #2. A child's chance to escape from "number 2" is close to zero.

Don't sugarcoat crime facts. Children, like adults, must face disturbing reality and learn to take risks quickly before it gets worse and too late. Sheltered children are the most vulnerable—worse, they're easy pickings for the scum in our society.

Part of the crime threat for children is confusion. During a crisis, confusion is often the first threat they experience. One way to break through the confusion is to explain clearly beforehand, "You do things differently when you are afraid and confused—everyday rules do not apply. You don't answer questions from strangers, you run away, you scream. Don't worry about being rude. When you're afraid and confused, it's okay."

Concerned that your children may overreact to a feeling

of fear and/or confusion? That's possible in the beginning, especially after learning something new and important. It's far better for children to be exposed early, react immediately, and risk overreaction than to do nothing. If children overreact to a feeling of fear, they'll learn from it. But if they're in danger and do nothing, you may lose them.

Encourage your children to listen and respond to their instincts instead of intellectualizing everything—something their parents probably do too much. For children, and adults, trusting your instincts is crucial to escaping violence. Children, like adults, can be very intuitive. However, if they're not encouraged to listen to their instincts, eventually they lose confidence in their gut feelings as well as their judgment and ability to make good decisions.

Most people, and especially children, are easily duped by experienced criminals because it's impossible always to discern well-meaning versus evil intentions on the part of strangers. Because children are sensitive and leery of being tricked or made to look foolish (which happens at home with older brothers and sisters and at school), they are often skeptical about everyone except their parents or teachers. Capitalize on this. By encouraging children to trust their instincts, they will be less afraid to act on any unexplained fears.

Children like to have their parents in charge, and they like to be a part of an organization, especially one like their family, that knows what to do and how to do it. It is a matter of security in a big world they are part of, but not in charge of. In their minds, most children place their parents in charge. It becomes a security issue for children to know they are part of a family that has an important plan. For children to commit themselves to being a part of a family escape-and-survive plan, they must have a role in that plan.

Don't assume that your older children know how to protect themselves against serious crime. The likelihood of violent crime of any sort occurring to our teenage and young adult children is skyrocketing because of their mobile lifestyle, lots of parties, juvenile risk-taking, and juveniles carrying concealed guns.

When I joined law enforcement in 1966, America averaged 350 kids accidentally killed per year from gun-related deaths . . . one kid per day. That figure remained stable for more than fifteen years. The key is, kids killed via guns used to be most often due to accidents at home or while hunting. That's all changed . . . dramatically. Not just the numbers, but from accident to murder. From 1984 to 1993, gun-related murders of juveniles increased fourfold . . . from an average of less than 400 to more than 1,700 (DOJ, 1995). In one city alone, Los Angeles, 150 kids per year are killed (accident and murder) by guns. In 1991, New York schools had the bloodiest year ever with 56 shootings; so, in the first two months of 1992, spot searches for guns were initiated. In one school alone, 121 guns were taken from high schoolers (from research by Bernard Furnish, professor, Westmont College).

The bottom line is that teenagers feel invulnerable, and we, as parents, need to help them make a reality check. We add to the problem by not insisting that our children face hard-line facts with us. However, I know this is a fact: that late-night phone call from a police officer at an emergency room will upset your family far more than if you had insisted your teenager listen to you about risks.

THE ESCAPE-AND-SURVIVE FAMILY DRILL

Remember, it's a family drill against an intruder or fire. The plan should be so direct that during a crisis when lives are threatened and you fear for one another, you'll all still be able to concentrate on escape.

In armed intrusion, the critical element is for the children to escape. Parents are more easily controlled when an intruder gets to a child and holds a weapon to him. It's far easier for children to get away and get help than for grown-ups because armed intruders always seek to control parents first, especially men.

Getting at least one person out of the home to get help will begin to break the control of an armed intruder, and it will likely be a child!

Everyone who lives at home must be together for the planning stage, no exceptions. Having everyone together is important for the adults, but it's crucial for the children. It demonstrates the importance of the plan and it helps give children the instruction and direction to leave their home and parents (which represent to them security in this world) to go for help, something their parents probably won't be able to do. Kids will think that getting out means abandoning the rest of the family unless you explain that because *they* escape for help, the police will come.

Make time to plan. Don't expect the process to be completed in one fifteen-minute period, especially with children involved. View your family's escape plan as a two-part plan: getting out, then getting help.

1. Go to every room, no matter how small—the walk-in closet, the bathroom without a window—every single one. You need to place in the children's minds the importance of making a decision on how to escape from that room if there's a window or door. From examining a walk-in closet or windowless bathroom, the child will know there's no way out, so he won't make the mistake of going there during an emergency.

Due to their inexperience and too much television, a child may pick a window eight feet high, and you will need to steer them toward another way out. Guide them toward good escape decisions, don't tell them. Every family member is to choose a door or a window to escape from in every room.

This room-by-room repetition cements the importance of escape when danger erupts. Because the whole family is participating, your children are again assured that everyone knows how to escape, reinforcing their self-permission to leave everyone and go for help.

Further, you're instilling in the child's mind not to run across the house to the one perfect escape spot. Depending on your home's layout, children should be able to get out of many rooms. This reduces the crucial seconds needed for eventual escape.

Going through the entire house room by room with everyone present, no matter how many different sessions this may take, is essential for families to effectively mind-set their escape. Parents are often quickly under the criminal's control; kids are often the family's last chance. Explain that every person in the family has an important job—kids really buy into this. Explain that if the children know how to escape, their parents will be less worried about them and this will help mom and dad concentrate on escaping themselves.

2. Choose a safety neighbor and one or two backups in case they aren't home. Your children need to feel that they made these choices with you. Instruct them clearly on what their job is and when it's finished:

• *They escape screaming and yelling.*
Screaming and yelling alerts other family members. It helps the child focus both mentally and physically on his escape and getting help. If they ask you, "What do I scream?" tell them, "Help! Help!" or "Fire! Fire!"

Rope

To escape from a second-story window and a few third-story windows, get a rope. (By the time you reach the fourth story, there's only one way out: the front door. The amount of rope needed would be far too massive.) My suggestion is regular old hemp-style cowboy rope (man-made fibers cut to the bone going down). Knot the rope every four to five feet (to make it easier to go down). Knots shorten a rope dramatically, so you must buy nearly double the length you need.

Secure the rope to something in the house: to the foot of a bed and then stuffed underneath; to hooks screwed into studs inside closets.

Rope vs. Rope Ladder

To cover the worst of situations, imagine your home being ravaged by fire or an intruder. You have your one-year-old in your arms. Will it be easier to go down a rope or rope-type ladder? Neither method will be easy because you will have only one hand free to hold the child, and you will be forced to go down in a half-gripping, half-sliding motion.

A rope ladder offers no advantages over a rope. You can lose your grip on both, but a ladder requires careful placing of your feet. If you miss a rung, you'll end up hanging upside down (I've seen it and I've done it in SWAT training) with your leg twisted above you, probably wrenched or broken, needing someone to rescue you.

A rope is less costly, requires far less storage space, and generally can reach farther down. It takes no more grip to slide down a rope than it does to hold on to a ladder. (Don't forget to knot it.) Most children are able to slide down a rope without a second thought. Going down a rope is easy; going up is the hard part.

- *They go to the safety neighbor screaming and yelling.*

Bang on the door, ring the doorbell. If no safety neighbor is at home, break a window, bringing attention or setting off an alarm. But they do not go into the home until the occupant responds.

- *Once contact is made, their job is finished, the child stays there.*

Knowing when their job is finished is important for children when they are afraid and confused. It will help them to concentrate.

One family I consulted with in upper New York State had no close neighbors; they chose a particular boulder for the children to go to that the entire family knew well. This choice gives the children an objective and denies the intruders the ability to use the children as a weapon against parents.

Clients in the Hollywood Hills went outside to choose a safety neighbor. The little boy said, "Dad, I've already decided how I'll get out of here." The estate was surrounded by high walls and high iron gates. The father said, "We designed this so that people can't get in. It's not possible for my son to get out." I asked the boy to show us. He took off like a deer and headed straight for one particular spot. He scaled the wall and was on the other side in seconds. His dad and I shook our heads.

As I've already said, mind-setting against one form of crime has additional value. Preparation against one crime leaves you prepared against other similar crimes. In the next story, a single mom prepared her two girls against a possible intruder, but the planning saved them from fire.

Susan Karsh, who went through training with me in 1983, asked to contribute her family's story. She said, "It might help other families understand how fast a crisis engulfs a family and puts their lives at risk."

Susan Karsh's Story

January 5, 1985. My two daughters and I were asleep upstairs. Around 1:45 A.M., something awakened me. I thought I smelled smoke, so I started down the stairs. Three steps down I could see flames through the smoke. I ran back up screaming, "Get up! Fire! Kristi, call 911!" They flew out of bed in a second. Kristi, fifteen, immediately went to the phone in my room. That was a mistake; we should have gotten out first, but at least we were all up and moving fast, not asking questions, not arguing, not wondering, "What now?" We had a plan, and that made the difference. It wasn't perfect; it had a few flaws, like calling before we escaped. But it was good enough to save us.

The fire was moving fast. The smoke was too thick to see across the room to the window. For the first time in my life, I felt real fear. My heart was pounding so hard I thought it would come through my chest. For a few seconds, I was paralyzed. Then I snapped out of it and grabbed Summer, my youngest. I pushed her face close to me and told her to breathe into my chest. She was crying. "We'll be okay," I said. The smoke was stifling. We were all choking and coughing.

I ran with Summer to the bathroom, slammed open the window, and shoved her out. "Breathe," I said. "I have to drop you like we talked about." I lowered her out the window, bending as much as I could to lessen the twenty-three-foot drop. She was screaming with fear but I told her, "I love you, Summer. You'll be all right. Roll out of the way when you hit. No matter how much you hurt, roll out of the way. Kristi's coming."

I let her go. At that point, I was so angry at everything. I didn't know how to save lives in a fire. I didn't know how to save lives period. I screamed to Kristi, "Throw down the phone! We have to get out now!" The window was only ten inches wide and she got stuck. I pushed her out, praying she would live through the fall. I heard her hit hard.

I was choking badly at this point. I couldn't get any air and I was getting dizzy. I yelled to my girls, "Go up to the street! Don't look back! No matter what, don't look back!" I thought for a second I wasn't going to make it. To this day, I don't know how, but I crawled out of the window and dropped. I don't remember going through the window or falling.

When you're older, you hit hard. I injured my back, broke my ankle, and cut my chin badly, but I flew up the embankment. I didn't even feel my broken ankle. Windows were blowing out behind me, one, then another.

When I reached the street, Kristi was busy alerting the neighbors. As we watched our home burn, Summer said to me, "It's okay, Mommy, you can lean on me. We're all safe now." I've never been more proud of my two girls.

At the hospital trauma center, the fire marshal said it was a miracle we got out. He said we must have practiced fire drills. It was then I realized that the way we got out was precisely the way we had practiced in case of an intruder, right down to going out the bathroom window. We chose that window because there was ground cover below to help cushion our fall.

We're alive because we had a plan. We were on automatic pilot. We didn't have time to confer. You must have a plan and practice that plan. Envision yourself in that situation; go through all the motions. We had practiced everything short of jumping out of the window.

It's critical not to have to begin from scratch. The fire marshal said I had only seconds left. If I had started out having to explain what to do and considering how best to get out, perhaps my daughters would have made it, but they wouldn't have a mom now because I would not have escaped. Those are the words of the fire marshal.

There's more to tell. A short time ago, Summer and I were leaving a restaurant in La Jolla, California. It was about eight in the evening, the streets were full of people—summertime. We were walking down the street arm in arm, giggling and laughing. Suddenly, out of the corner of my eye, I saw this horrible-looking person lunging at me, shrieking at the top of his voice. A street person, obviously deranged and a Charles Manson look-alike. He was screaming, "Don't talk to me that way, bitch!" He came at me and tried to hit me with a doubled fist. It happened fast. I pushed Summer to the side. I didn't have time to say anything, but we had talked about it before, so she knew what to do. She took off like a little bullet down the street. I was running right after her. She didn't wait to see what I was going to do. We had to jump over a planter box. Summer slammed into it and hurt her hip, but she didn't cry, just got back up and kept running. Later she said she remembered that I had told her she might get hurt. I am so proud of her.

Sometimes I think this incident was trivial compared to the fire, but others have pointed out that Summer and I could have been beaten or stabbed by this street crazy.

I truly believe the time that my daughters and I have spent talking about how to protect ourselves will continue to make a difference in their lives as they go off to school, work, and have their own families.

What the Karshes Did Wrong

Susan has said it herself, "We were fixed on calling 911, which may not be wrong in an intruder situation. But with a fire, I know now the priority is to get out first and then call for help from a neighbor's."

My preference for the family escape-and-survive plan is to have more than one window for everyone to go out of, especially because one particular window may not be accessible in all emergencies. They would have been better off with an alternative escape via a knotted rope from another window.

What the Karshes Did Right

Susan Karsh, a single working mother, made the time in her schedule to create a family escape plan with her two daughters and to practice it with them. This preparation gave them survival decisions to fall back on. No doubt it saved a life.

Visualize these two separate scenes. One is a family with a personal family escape plan against fire and intruders, the other family without an escape plan.

The first family: The intruders have entered the home. They first desperately try to get everyone under control and in one room. But instead of freezing up in shock, disbelief, paralyzed with fear, this family has one aim—discussed and practiced. Each family member has one job and only one: children to escape, adults helping, pushing, screaming at others to get out, then adults getting out. Scared? *You bet they're scared.* But, there is a difference in being scared versus paralyzed with shock and fear. They're screaming, shattering windows—nothing compares to smashing a window when you want to alert people or bring pressure on others, like intruders. Will everyone get out? Maybe not. Will anyone be injured? Probably. But, if one person, such as a child with a strong sense of duty to the family's escape-and-survive plan, escapes to a safety neighbor, the time for crimes will be drastically reduced from hours to minutes. Too much responsibility placed on children? I don't believe so. Especially when considering our purpose, what we're trying to stop, what we're trying to save.

The second family: Without any preparation they face an

intruder. Control will be immediate, I promise you. Family members bound is the most probable. Next, mothers and daughters raped is also probable. Senseless beatings, perhaps worse. Robbery will be the least of the crimes. They will finally leave, but only when they are through with everyone.

A crime attack and the crime aftermath are two very different things. When the crimes and the violence against people are over and the criminals are gone, the ordeal for victims is *just beginning.*

Reality-based mind-setting is the heart of surviving violence for all ages. If you have children, they need to know there is good and bad in the world, and when they face the bad, the outcome will largely depend on what they do. So gather your family, lead them.

Part VI

Six Ways to a Safer Future

There are six changes that will bring about a safer future. Some will be immediate, some longer in coming; at the very least, they will provide that our children and grandchildren don't live with the same level of violence we now experience.

Three Long-Term Ways

1. GUNS—FIVE CRITERIA BEFORE LOADING

Guns are a part of America and they're not going away. The Department of Justice reports 40 percent of Americans admit having guns in their home. Research by both the NRA and their adversary Handgun Control Inc. shows that gun ownership is much higher; at least another 20 percent have guns at home and don't talk about it.

There has been a dramatic increase in gun ownership since the 1960s. Handgun ownership alone is up 200 percent. Because people are scared. Violent crime has increased 300 percent since the mid-1960s. A spokesman for the Law Enforcement Alliance of America said, "These people are not all gun lovers. Most are just people who want an insurance policy."

The problem is not the widespread availability of guns, it's education. There is no longer a prerequisite of knowledge, efficiency, pride, attached to gun ownership—only a "fear" prerequisite. As recently as thirty years ago, most gun owners were hunters, marksmen, farmers and ranchers, or collectors; people who had experienced knowledge and respect for a gun. Now, most gun buyers operate solely out of fear; their only interest is, how do I load it?

Frankly, many new gun owners believe that buying the gun, loading it, pointing it, and pulling the trigger is enough—that the gun will then take care of business. They're as wrong as the people who believe guns are the source of violence. Guns cannot in themselves protect people from violence any more than they can initiate violence.

A female attorney told me, "I have a gun at home, but I've never shot it—would you show me how?" We met at the firing range, and she shot thirty to forty rounds. I suggested we talk about what it would take from her to, at close range, use it against a man. She didn't want to discuss it. She's an armed woman due to fear, and to her credit, doing something about it, but unless she's done more than that one hour on the range, she's not safe and effective, too. With that limited experience, no one can be ready to kill a man at close range in self-defense unless it's their lucky day.

The average gun owner with protection in mind fires thirty or forty bullets from a fifty-bullet box of pistol ammunition. That leaves enough bullets to go home, load up, and believe they're ready for a gunfight in their living room. They're not.

In America, we can't discuss protection against home intruders without discussing "home guns." In this story, the homeowner is a cop. A cop's oath of office directs him to react against serious crime far differently from a citizen. That's why many policemen, including the one in this story, don't try to escape when trouble confronts them. I'm

---

In America, two events escalate the purchase of guns more than any others:

1. A riot. During and immediately following the 1992 riot in South Central Los Angeles (the worst in U.S. history), gun stores were cleaned out — by looters as well as legitimate buyers. More handguns were sold during and in the weeks following the riot than altogether in the five previous years.
2. Any hint of federal restrictions to gun ownership. One gunshop owner said he sold every handgun he had when the semiautomatic handgun bill was being debated. It was his biggest single rush of business.

---

including this account to emphasize how dangerous con-
fronting an armed intruder can be—even for a cop.

Bob Connaughy's Story

March 26, 1985, 9:30 A.M. My wife was at work and I was
the only one at home when I heard the doorbell ring. I
got dressed and walked to the kitchen window and saw a
car parked across the street with two men standing next
to it, glancing about. Then they started walking toward
my house. It didn't take me long to add two and two:
someone was going to be burglarized—me or a neighbor.
I immediately called my substation and told the operator,
"I need patrol units fast."

I got out my .45 and went to the hallway.

It seemed like less than a minute after the doorbell
rang, suddenly I heard something hit one of the windows
at the rear of the house. Then, a couple more hits and I
could hear the window break.

I'm here to tell you, my nerves were peaked. I had
never planned out in my mind having to take a crook
down inside my own home. On duty, I'd done it many
times and, like any cop, had planned it all in my mind.
Having done that for work made the initial difference for
me at home. It helped me concentrate.

A hand reached through the broken window, opened
it, and a man climbed in. The guy went directly to our
sliding glass door and let his partner in. It was
unbelievable how fast they were getting in.

My thinking time was over. I made my move. I stepped
around the corner in the hallway, pointed my weapon at
them, and shouted, "On the ground!"

The one who had come through the window hit the
floor like a pancake. The second intruder ducked back
out the sliding glass door and was gone. The one on the
floor had a twelve-inch screwdriver in his hand. Twelve

inches of stabbing tool—I've seen the damage they do. "Drop the screwdriver!" I shouted. I crouched and inched toward him. He was still "proned out." I grabbed the screwdriver shaft in my left hand.

I didn't want to shoot him. Through the whole thing, I didn't want to shoot him. This was a lesson I'll never forget: hesitation. I'll never repeat that mistake.

He had a death grip on his screwdriver. I let go and stepped back. Again I ordered him, "Drop it!" He said, "I'm nervous. I can't." I said, "I'm a cop, drop it or I'll shoot."

"I have three friends outside," he said. Then, he slowly got up into a crouch. He was damned experienced. He sensed my reluctance to shoot him.

I backed up several feet. What am I going to do? Should I shoot him? All that was racing through me. At this point, I had backed up maybe eight feet into the corner, still telling him, "Drop it or I'll shoot."

Then, he made his move. He growled and lunged at me. I blocked his first attempt to stab me. We were inches apart. He was on me. I still didn't want to shoot him. I moved my gun back and close to my body, trying to keep it out of his reach—training instincts were taking over. Then, he brought his arm back to stab again. It raced through me—you've had one try at me; you don't get two. I fired.

Damn, nothing happened. I had the gun into his stomach point-blank when I pulled the trigger. Nothing. He didn't go down.

I fired again. This time he went down hard. I backed up and turned to the sliding glass door. I was still worried about his buddies. When I turned, he jumped up, threw open the front door, and ran out right through the screen door. I took off after him, but then turned back to call 911.

Later that day units found him at the hospital with one .45 wound in his belly. My first shot had hit his belt buckle and ricocheted off. My second shot entered next to his belly button, went all the way through and out his butt. And he still took off like a rabbit.

Looking back, I gave him the advantage and an opportunity to take me out. He tried twice. That morning changed me. Never again will I hesitate.

I also feel more for citizens now. It was a close call. If I had not been trained to handle an attack, I think he would have taken me out. Even with my training, I was still nervous and tense as hell. Most citizens would have bought it.

I had a plan, but it was flawed. I hadn't worked out in my mind how I would handle something like this in my own home. I knew what I wanted to do, but I hadn't decided what I wouldn't do and wouldn't let happen. I had not told myself, don't get close to him, don't let him back you up, don't give him the time he needs to get to you. I had not made the decision about when I would shoot in my own home. My strategy is different now, I've got a new plan. Beginning with, "I won't make it so easy to kill me. If there is a next time in my home, when I say drop the weapon, it better happen fast."

In those final seconds, with him inches away from me and on the attack, that's when I was no longer thinking; the academy trainers were right. There's no thinking and no planning—you fall back on training.

What Bob Did Wrong

Like most police officers I've known, Bob had not made the critical "shoot/no-shoot" decision against an intruder in his own home. His reluctance to use deadly force, especially off duty at home, is typical of cops and costs some of them their lives.

What Bob Did Right

Although a cop himself, Bob first called the police, then made a crucial mental switch from routine home activities to a survival mind-set. At that instant, he, like everyone else, fell back on training.

For the Record

Bob said a citizen faced with these same circumstances would probably have "bought it."

I agree. The intruder got five years.

Note: In any violent attack, but especially in a home, if you're both armed, the one who waits too long probably doesn't get a round off or does it with a bullet already in him. I've never been around a police officer or citizen who, after using a gun against an intruder, didn't say, "It was the worst experience and closest call of my life."

What if the same attack happens to you? Escape! Get out! Your job is to protect your family, not society. You're not trained or paid to risk bringing in crooks. If escape is not possible, that's different. Having a loaded gun at home has saved many lives but, unfortunately, cost many, too.

Citizens who are armed but not safe and also effective are the first part of the problem. The second part of the problem are the so-called "home-defense strategies" being promoted. Some so-called professionals advise people on how to arm themselves and clear their home of intruders. I've never met a sane professional who would advise anyone to clear his home of intruders. It's what we in law enforcement used to call the "cowboy" approach, used to describe someone who is kind of riding in half-saddled, shooting from the hip with both guns blazing. This is a typical example of cowboy advice I read in a magazine: "Be careful not to expose yourself to areas that have not been cleared. Instead, let the muzzle of your gun precede you into the danger area." The illustration depicts a man clearing a bedroom and then a closet. The author remarks, "Safety resides at the end of your muzzle." That's like hoping the gun has eyes that can see if there's anything in the closet. It's too dangerous to deal with a possible intruder like this, and it's a good way to have your gun taken away from you. The writer goes on to say, "The most important thing is being prepared to shoot all the time."

What I see building here is tragedy—the potential of accidentally shooting the wrong person. I remember a case involving a father and a .357 magnum. He had established safety rules for his family. He told his family that if he screamed, "Intruder!" they were to hide so they wouldn't distract him. He should have said, "Escape!" He also did something excellent that few gun owners do: he never left the gun loaded in the house when he wasn't home, but unfortunately, it wasn't enough.

One early morning, his four-year-old son woke up and went to the bathroom. Another rule in this family was that the children had to knock first and announce themselves before entering their parents' bedroom. The father had heard some noise down the hall, and when he heard the doorknob to his bedroom being fiddled with, he grabbed his gun and aimed at the door. The father said, "I aimed low so I wouldn't kill the man." Unfortunately, his low shot put a bullet through his son's upper chest and neck. His son died.

This man was awakened from a deep sleep, was disoriented, slow to react, thickheaded. Not the best time to grab a loaded gun and aim it at the door thinking, "I'll blow away anyone who comes through it."

Clearing a house of intruders is fraught with problems and danger. Problems such as, "Do I turn on the lights, ruin my night vision, maybe expose myself, and shoot into the dark when something moves? Or do I yell, 'I have a gun,' hoping to scare off the intruder? Or is yelling letting him know where I am so he can shoot at me? Which room do I check first, and how do I check it?"

When a homeowner hears an unidentified noise in his home that gut fear tells him might be an intruder, it's foolish for him to search his home trying to find the noise. I've never known of any sane police officer trying to clear a house or building of possible burglars or intruders by himself. It doesn't matter how well you know your home. It doesn't work in real life the way it looks on paper and in pictures. Every house or business I've ever cleared, I cleared in the company of other cops.

Family survival planning should concentrate on escape, never on seeking out and outgunning intruders. I am not against guns or gun ownership. Far from it. But I am against using loaded home guns as the only means of family protection against intruders.

The problem is not gun ownership or gun control. The problem is that loaded guns at home do not effectively protect most families against armed intruders. Not because guns are ineffective—but because some *people* with guns are ineffective and dangerous. Period.

In America:

- Eighty-three percent of suicides by gun are committed with a firearm kept primarily for home protection.
- Ten percent of all loaded guns kept in American homes for protection end up being used to kill a family member during the heat of an argument.
- On average, one child per day is killed while playing with a loaded gun.

In 1985, the *New England Journal of Medicine* published a study of gun deaths in the private homes of King County, Washington. During the five years between 1978 and 1983, 396 people were killed by firearms in private residences.

Some were children playing with guns, some were husbands and wives killed in marital disputes, others were suicides. How many were intruders shot by homeowners using a loaded gun for family or personal protection (the primary reason for most guns to be loaded at home)? *Two!*

Another tragic consequence of loaded guns at home is that criminals often seize the weapons and use them against the homeowner. It happens to cops, whose greatest fear is that in a scuffle their gun might be taken away and used against them. Cops receive training to keep this from happening; they think about it, practice against it, and plan against it. Yet too frequently officers are still disarmed and killed or wounded. It almost happened to me twice, and I assure you, it happens to citizens.

But, as disturbing as the preceding facts on accidental deaths are, most home guns in the hands of responsible, knowledgeable owners are never used except in a life-threatening emergency.

Gary Kleck, a professor at Florida State University, wrote *Point-Blank* in 1991. His groundbreaking research has startled many on both sides of the gun debate: "In one year alone, 1980, between 1,527 and 2,819 criminals were killed by citizens in their personal defense . . . while between 1967 and 1984, only twenty murderers were executed after conviction for killing citizens. . . . Violence-prone intruders realize that death is more likely to come from armed homeowners than the criminal justice system."

Sociologists James Wright and Peter Rossi, both regularly quoted in criminal-violence research programs, report, "Three-fifths of all felons interviewed said they are more worried over running into armed citizens than running into the police."

The Department of Justice Uniform Crime Reports and National Crime Victimization survey show that "guns are used about as often for defensive purposes as criminal purposes."

According to Professor Kleck, there were "691,000 defensive gun uses in America between 1985 and 1990."

Marjorie Casey's Story

In 1988, when my daughter went away to college, I arranged to buy a condominium closer to town in La Jolla. As a last-minute thing, the owner (who, it turned out, didn't really own it) asked to rent one of the rooms upstairs for himself and his three-year-old daughter until he could relocate (I had met the little girl). It was a large three-bedroom condo and they would be there less than a month. I didn't see anything wrong with his request and he paid the rent I asked.

Thirty days passed and he stonewalled me every time I brought up our agreement that he would move out. I was getting uneasy. Then it turned out the little girl was not his daughter but the child of a relative who had been incarcerated. It was getting worse. Creditors started coming to the condo looking for him, and I realized he was a scam artist.

I became frightened. The police could not help me because I had authorized him to stay as a renter and it would take time to evict him. He had not done anything the police could arrest him for—I checked. I felt trapped. I had no agency to turn to and nowhere else to live. It was clear I had to confront him and tell him to leave.

I remember the day I was going to tell him he must leave. I was in my office in the spare bedroom and a sense of danger went through me that I couldn't explain. I went to my closet and unpacked the gun my father had given me, loaded it, and placed it in my pocket. I knew how to use it. Our family had been ranchers. I had never done anything like that before. Looking back, I guess I was finally listening to my instincts.

When he returned that day, I told him, "You need to find another place to live immediately. I'm aware of your scams." He immediately turned very profane and threatening. It was like a switch from Jekyll to Hyde.

"You bitch!" he shouted, then he started slamming the wall with his fist.

I had never been around violence before. I just freaked and I pulled out the gun.

He was a few feet from me, yelling, "Fuck you, bitch!" He lunged at me.

I pulled the trigger—hit him twice. He kept coming. I know it happened in a split second, but it seemed like slow motion.

He slugged me in the head and tried to take the gun from me. I held on to it. We fell backward into the television and table, knocking everything over as we fell. I was screaming. He was shouting, "I'll kill you, bitch!" He was on top of me, straddling me. He had one hand on my gun, the other hand hitting and choking me. Then the worst happened. He wrestled the gun from me, held it to my face . . . *click*. It didn't fire.

He hit me in the head with the gun, choked me, and slugged me over and over. Suddenly, something in me switched—my fear changed to hate. I exploded. I was insane with madness. I struck back, biting, kicking, and screaming. I got him off me and flew down the stairs and ran out the door. A carpet cleaner in a nearby condo called 911. The police finally arrived and took me to the hospital. The man died.

What Marjorie Did Wrong

Marjorie says, "Aside from the obvious mistake I made—allowing him to rent from me—there is another mistake I will never again make: that's not listening to my gut instinct when he began stonewalling me."

The confrontation was necessary but could have been better planned. She should have chosen a different location, preferably not a small enclosed space, and asked someone to accompany her for support. In hindsight, at the very least Marjorie would have had a witness.

What Marjorie Did Right

Marjorie finally listened to her gut instinct and took protective measures against a potential danger in her own home.

Because of previous training that focused on her ability to concentrate, she was able to use her firearm effectively at a critical distance under extreme conditions.

For the Record

Marjorie was the victim; nonetheless, she was charged with murder because she knew the man and had armed herself ahead of time. She was found guilty of involuntary manslaughter which carries the least severe sentencing for a shooting incident such as this with loss of life. She was given five years' probation without any time behind bars.

Note: I've seen many cases like this one where a woman faces potential violence from a man and the police are powerless to intervene. In America, 30 to 35 percent of all women murder victims are killed by ex-husbands, husbands, boyfriends, or people well known to them.

Even though Marjorie was familiar with guns and didn't miss, she was still overpowered and her gun was used against her. It was pure luck that the gun jammed.

A fact often misunderstood by people who decide to use guns for protection is one or more bullets seldom instantly stop an attacker. More often, even when hit with multiple bullets, a mortally wounded attacker is still able to reach, grab, struggle with, and often disarm the shooter, with far more physical power available to him than he normally would have.

Marjorie is alive because she didn't accept helplessness. Nor did she give up when the police didn't intervene. Most important, she didn't give up when he overpowered her, wrenched and twisted the gun from her, injuring her hand badly, choked her, and hit her face over and over with the steel of the gun.

Instead, Marjorie reacted to everything as most men would. The double-standard: young men are conditioned to be self-reliant; young women are conditioned to seek help. The result for most women is that they are not prepared to face death, mentally or physically, and survive. Relying on the police or others to save you is gambling big-time. We usually get there too late.

So, that's the sobering news about loaded guns for personal protection—over 90 percent of them in homes. And the bottom line is unchanged: the difference between being armed versus armed, safe, and effective is big-time.

A lot of people know a little about guns, some know a lot about guns, but few know anything about using guns at critical distances and under deadly conditions.

Using a gun or not using one is your decision. But if you want to include a gun in your family's protection plan, you must know how to use it effectively and safely. You need to go beyond just being armed. That means meeting the following criteria before loading up.

The Five Criteria for Having a Loaded Gun for Protection

One: You Load It—You're Responsible

Loaded guns in private homes are virtually always kept solely for personal or family protection. If you make this choice (to keep a loaded gun at home), you are personally responsible for everything having to do with that weapon, twenty-four hours a day. When you load a gun, you are responsible for unloading it. That includes making certain the gun is unloaded while you're not at home. The objective is not to make a loaded gun readily available for accidents or criminal use.

That's right. You must load and unload it *every day* before leaving for work or even just the corner market. No exceptions. A hassle, yes, but cheap insurance against a dead child. If you're unloading a semiautomatic handgun—remember, it's *the magazine plus one.* Forgetting that *plus one,* the bullet still in the chamber, is the reason many children are dead.

I predict laws in America will and should swing toward "you load it—you're responsible for it." We already hold bartenders and private hosts responsible for serving drunks who are later involved in drunk-driving collisions.

Two: Know the Gun—Inside and Out

Get expert firearms instruction and experience from a professional. Become a good marksman, not just a gun owner. You must gain confidence and competence with your firearm before learning how to use it to save your life. For example, too many new gun owners cannot clear jams in semiautomatic handguns in daylight, let alone in complete darkness and under greater stress than they've ever before experienced. A box or two of ammunition and a couple of trips to the shooting range or back country is not enough. No one has or maintains shooting skills without practice.

Who is an expert instructor? Ask yourself, "Will I get the best training from someone who has had hands-on experi-

---

A recent article in the *New York Times* cited a case in Missouri City, Texas: "After some friends persuaded him that it was a good idea, Sam Walker bought a .38-caliber revolver several weeks ago, to protect his family and home in this Houston suburb. Mr. Walker says he did not like guns and, until Monday, had never even fired one." That was when his burglar alarm went off in the middle of the day and he got his gun. He saw a figure moving and fired in a microsecond. He shot his sixteen-year-old daughter, who was skipping school.

---

ence using firearms under deadly conditions or from someone who has read about it?" To teach students who want to
be prepared to use a firearm for self-preservation, the
instructor needs experience beyond the firing range. In
combination, expert instruction, a sound understanding of
firearms, and good marksmanship form are your critical
first step in using guns safely and effectively to save your
life.

Three: Point-of-Aim

After becoming a competent firearms handler and marksman comes point-of-aim shooting (shooting to save your
life). It was first introduced by the Marine Corps in the mid-
sixties; we called it *quick-kill.* Later, some SWAT trainers
changed the term to *instinct shooting.* Most experienced
trainers now refer to this skill as *point-of-aim* or *point
shooting.* It's not sport shooting or basic marksmanship. It's
learning the skill necessary to shoot at a human being who
is threatening your life at close range. At any close-in
distance you will not have time to use your sights or any
other basic marksmanship training. Trying to use the sights
of your gun under life-or-death conditions at close distances
is unnatural, nearly impossible, and dangerous.

This is a brief summary of point-of-aim shooting, which
relies on the human body's natural ability to point instantly
with accuracy. (What follows is not a substitute for hands-
on instruction.) Successful point-of-aim shooting is an
intense mind-and-body concentration on one small point in
the middle of your target (police officers call that spot the
10-ring). With one or both hands (I prefer both), thrust
your weapon toward the target. Fix your eyes, your mind,
every muscle—total concentration on the 10-ring. Peripher-
ally, your eyes see your thrust-out gun barrel. Because
optically, physically, and mentally you are concentrated on
the same spot, you will automatically adjust the gun barrel
for that spot.

Marksmanship requires a *relaxed* concentration involving breathing, stance, relaxation of your eyes and muscles, and sight alignment with your target. Point-of-aim is *intense* concentration on just the 10-ring.

Surviving a critical-incident shooting doesn't depend on who has the most bullets, the biggest gun, the longest barrel, or even on who is the best marksman. It depends on superior concentration for a few split seconds. No way around this: intense concentration separates the winners and losers in a close-in deadly exchange of gunfire. The slightest distraction returns every advantage to the bad guy. Big difference in marksmanship training and point-of-aim training. Be sure your instructor has point-of-aim experience. With rare exception, point-of-aim experience begins with law enforcement and/or military backgrounds.

Four: Can You Kill a Man?

Be honest with yourself: Are you ready to kill another person? I didn't say "ready to threaten" an intruder. I said, "Are you ready to kill someone you believe is threatening your life?" It will go something like this:

You will not be a safe distance away. You'll be close, real close, because it will likely be inside your home. Count on approximately five feet, but maybe only inches. The fight will be one-on-one—possibly to the death for one or both of you. To stop him, you'll probably have to shoot him more than once because he'll be close enough to use his weapon on you, even while you're shooting him. Don't expect him to turn and run after one shot, whether you hit him or not. Don't expect a clean, one-hit stop. Expect screaming. Expect everything to be blood-soaked, including you, your own blood and likely his, too. Even if he is badly wounded, expect him to get to you or perhaps a family member, maybe with his weapon still in his hands.

Count on this: You can be completely familiar with guns

and still find criminal assault a complete shock. Violent attacks are never clean and seldom go down or end the way you hope or expect. They're unforgettable. *They will change your life forever.*

Include in your survival plan exactly what you will say as well as what you will order him to do or not do. Make it brief. For twenty years, I yelled the same words every time: "Freeze or you're a dead man!"

You will be face-to-face with someone ready to kill you. He has probably killed before—criminal recidivism statistics bear that out. Using hesitant, uncertain words—"I don't want to shoot you"; "Don't make me shoot you"; "Please leave and no one will get hurt"—will likely lead to your gun's being yanked away and used against you. Be forceful and clear—leave no doubt in his mind what he must do to avoid deadly consequences.

When do you shout orders, versus when do you use a gun? At no time is concentration more critical than when making a shoot/no-shoot decision. Make your "I'll squeeze the trigger when . . . " decision ahead of time.

Five: Escape—Don't Make a Gun Your Center of Survival

Don't make a gun your sole means of escape, and especially don't make it the sole means of protection for your family. Establish the family escape-and-survive plan, and use the methods I outlined to teach your children how to escape crime. Then, if an intruder strikes when you're home and if your gun is close by, fine. But, first *concentrate on escape with your family.* Use your gun to ensure your escape. Never choose to stand your ground and shoot it out instead of escaping. Under ideal conditions, the best marksmen in the world have a fifty-fifty chance to shoot the other guy first in gun battles when the shooters are separated by a few feet. Remember that trained police officers hit suspects only once out of every four shots at three to nine feet.

When I was a new police officer working alone, one night about eleven-thirty, I saw two men walking and got a feeling about them. I decided to shake 'em down. They both took off. I chased after one, gun in hand. He ducked into an alley. As I turned the corner, he jumped me. We went down, rolling on the sidewalk. He had both hands on my gun. I had one arm around his neck, my other on my gun. I was one all-alone-and-scared cop, fearing my gun would be used against me.

"Concentrate on the gun barrel. Keep it away from you and on him. The gun barrel! Concentrate. Concentrate!" The police trainers' words instantly filled my mind.

We were both screaming. He was yanking at my gun and I was holding on for dear life. Then he started pleading, "You're choking me." I eased up on my headlock. Big mistake. He pulled at my gun with renewed power. I let go of his neck and grabbed my gun with both hands. Now there were four hands on the gun. He pushed it toward me — hard. I pushed back. "Get the barrel on him." I got the barrel on him for just a second and pulled the trigger. (From the instant I got out of my car to the moment I shot him, the whole incident took fifteen to twenty seconds. It goes down fast.)

Blood was pouring from his shoulder. He went dead silent for three or four seconds, then he began a high-pitched screaming that sounded just like a wounded rabbit. I got scared about internal bleeding and that he might die on me. So I cuffed him (so he couldn't struggle against me) and carried him over my shoulder back to my car. I strapped him into the front seat, called the dispatcher to have officers meet me at the hospital, and took off, driving with one hand while pressing on his wound with the other. He never stopped screaming. We were both blood soaked. He lived.

If you drop the gun or it is wrestled away from you or it is not close enough to reach in an instant—forget the gun. Focus only on escape. Be disciplined and in control enough to shift from getting a gun, or getting it back, to escape.

Meet all five criteria or unload. And, *keep* meeting all five criteria. Law enforcement officers, our nation's experts at using firearms at critical distances under deadly conditions, have annual refresher training, and in some cities, semiannually. SWAT teams generally have firearms training weekly to twice a month at the very least.

A tragic and life-threatening difference between armed citizens and cops: by huge percentages, armed citizens use a gun in their defense far more than cops. Yet, cops, who cannot be there when violence strikes, are the ones with specialized training for a life-or-death armed confrontation. Worse, unlike cops, citizens do not get the benefit of critiquing a shooting and learning what was right and wrong about their handling of the confrontation—except in a newspaper. The bottom-line problem: Cops are the only ones who have a method to learn from right and wrong actions. The solution: Use these five criteria, not only in your goal of being more than just armed, but as your method of critique of another's armed confrontation.

Adopt this decision for your family: Our objective is to escape to survive. This gun is simply insurance that no one blocks our escape. If our family faces violence like a home intrusion, the cleaner and less entangled our escape is, the happier we'll be when we look back on it.

Mind-setting against crime is the heart of crime survival. Having a gun in your hands and pointing it at an intruder doesn't change that fact. With or without a gun, your mind-set will make the difference.

George Copetas's Story

August 1976. I've been around guns all of my life—rifles, shotguns, pistols. I'm a collector. One night I was helping out in a family-owned liquor store in the Point Loma area of San Diego, and I stashed my gun under the register. Liquor store clerks and taxi drivers are second only to cops for being targets.

The store had a floor mat at the entrance that rang a bell when a customer stepped on it. Right in front of that was an ice-cream freezer. That's where I was—rearranging the ice cream.

Suddenly I felt a breeze. I turned around and saw him. He had jumped over the mat so it wouldn't ring. He was wearing panty hose over his head, a watch cap, and a plaid shirt buttoned to the top. He had gloves on, and of course he had a gun, a Beretta.

"Give me all the money or I'll blow your fucking head off." Those were his exact words. I wasn't too frantic at that time because the hammer was down. In those days, Berettas were not double-action automatics. The hammer had to be physically pulled back, cocked before he could fire it. So I knew I had at least a second or two. I tried to settle him down: "Hey, don't worry, the money is insured."

I had played out in my mind being robbed: I would simply give him the money and he would walk out. Because I kept my gun behind the counter next to the cash register, I would wait until he got near the front door, pull my gun, and say, "Okay, now drop the money and get the hell out of here or we're going to have a problem." I had even planned what I would say. The cash register would be my shield, my cover. Those were my thoughts. He's going to be over there—fifteen feet away. I'm going to be safe behind the cash register. A perfect-for-me scenario.

The real thing was different. He walked around the counter with me. "Shit," I remember saying to myself. He's going to see everything, including my gun. He looked quickly but didn't see it. He said, "Hurry up, put all the money in a bag and give it to me or I'll blow your fucking head off." Second time he said that. He seemed to be getting nervous—the gun was inches from my head.

I started pulling the money out to give him and I activated a silent alarm to the police department at the same time. He reached around behind me for my wallet. I said I only keep credit cards there. "Shut up or I'll blow your fucking head off," he said again.

A customer walked in. "You—get down on the floor, put your hands over your head, straight out, look straight down. Don't move!" That customer could have ducked back out the door, but he froze up. He hit the deck, fast.

Getting the money together took seconds but seemed like forever. Finally he had all the money and we were facing each other, maybe three feet apart. The gun was only inches away. Then he cocked it.

"Shit, he's going to shoot me! I did what he wanted and the bastard is going to kill me anyway." I was scared to death but I knew what I had to do—get my gun. If I didn't, I knew it was over for me. "Distract him" was racing through my mind. I said, "Hey, wait a minute. I've got more money, you want it?" "Yeah, yeah, hurry up or I'll blow your fucking head off." I told him, "It's under the counter."

I can see him to this day. I was down on one knee looking up at him, his gun inches from my face. Right between my eyes, and cocked. I put my hand under the counter. I could feel my gun, finally! A double-action Smith & Wesson .38. I didn't have to cock it, just pull the trigger. I was ready.

Suddenly a feeling of cold contempt and hatred for the

bastard ran through me. I knew he was going to kill me. He had cocked that Beretta. It doesn't take a mental giant to know what's ahead when a man has you on your knees, a gun on you, and he cocks it.

He was looking down at me and over to the customer on the floor and at the same time trying to watch the door. He's going to execute me, I could feel it.

He moved the gun slightly from between my eyes toward my ear and then back to my eyes. I prayed. I remember it clearly. "I hate to do this, Lord, but I'm asking—push that gun off my head once more, then I'm going to shoot him. It's me or him. Please, Lord, one more time, please let it go right for me."

At that instant, that SOB moved the gun a fraction off my head. I pulled out my gun and rammed it into his gut and emptied it into him before he knew what happened. No aiming—just pulling the trigger. He went, "Huh," then his hands came to his chest. He dropped his gun. He spun around and went down—on the floor, on his knees with his head down. But he wasn't finished. His gun was on the floor next to him, still cocked.

I rushed to the phone. Then I saw the customer still lying on the floor. He was shaking from head to foot, just shivering, looking straight down. I said, "Hey, it's okay, you can get up. I shot him." He turned over, looked at me, moaned a little, then urinated on himself. Poor guy, probably came in for a six-pack.

I called the police and went back near the robber. I couldn't believe it. He was groaning, still alive. Six of my bullets in his chest and stomach and he's hanging on. I got scared all over again. His gun was close to him, still cocked. He's coughing up blood but still able to move. I didn't want to touch his gun or get my fingerprints on it, so I reloaded my gun. Then I was looking at him. Should I shoot him again? What if he goes for his gun? Shit, this is not at all the way I thought it would happen.

Thank the Lord, the police showed up, coming from all directions. The first officer in the store, when he saw my gun, drew on me. I threw my gun on the counter and said, "No, no," and pointed to the robber. I'll never forget the scene. There was blood coming from his back, his gut, and his mouth. It was a bloody mess. We found blood on the liquor bottles for weeks. He died there, on the floor.

What George Did Wrong

George had a plan in place should he be robbed or his life threatened. However, like most plans, his was based on circumstances entirely favorable to him and didn't account for the worst case (wishful optimism is not atypical for emergency plans). Being on his knees with a gun at his head was not part of George's plan.

What George Did Right

Because George had a plan, he was able to think clearly and to improvise his way into action — he figured out a way to get his hand on his own gun.

Because of his familiarity with guns, he knew what he was up against.

George had already made the crucial "I'll shoot when . . ." decision. Because of that, and his concentration, George didn't wait to find out if the man holding him at gunpoint would execute him or not.

Two bottom lines to consider:

1. You're better off not pulling the trigger unless you can justify the shot by this standard: deadly force was your only chance to save your life or the lives of others, and you can articulate that in court. No warning shots — innocent bystanders are too often the victims.
2. There's nothing wrong in asking this question: "Am I ready to kill a man?" That question shows intelligence and nothing less. If your honest answer is no, don't complicate, don't

obstruct, your escape and survival with a gun. Any armed man or woman who faces a violent criminal is also facing life-or-death decisions that will be made in split seconds, and their mind will also be cluttered with intense emotions.

In every gun incident I've been in, I was scared and physically shook when it was over. George Copetas says, "I still get a chill up my spine thinking about it and I'm still angry that I had to kill him."

I've had an objective with this section on guns beyond teaching: to make your decision to rely on a gun a difficult one, so that people choosing guns will be only those who truly need a firearm and as a result will truly prepare themselves beyond just being armed.

Extreme political positions have turned "guns" into a heated, complex issue. No organization has more experience with gun safety and the effective use of firearms than the National Rifle Association. As a matter of fact, that's why it was formed in the first place. During the Civil War, Union military leaders found that Union troops were far less accurate with their rifles than Confederate troops, and they feared that had it not been for the South's lack of material resources, the Confederates might have won the war due to better marksmanship. So the NRA was formed in the North to improve the marksmanship of Union troops.

The NRA's mandate for over a century has been hands-on education in the safe and effective use of firearms. Its leadership in gun safety has resulted in a 56 percent decrease in fatal gun accidents since the 1930s in spite of a quadrupling in gun ownership of all types of guns.

But, today, the NRA has moved beyond its original mission of gun knowledge and safety. The result for both the NRA and its enemies is extreme positions on both sides that are nondefensible. For example, the NRA does not logically defend the need to own "street-sweepers" and cheap Saturday-night specials, nor can the extreme faction of the gun-control groups logically defend any restriction on law-abiding citizens legally buying guns. The 300 percent increase in violence since the mid sixties is solely attributable to recidivism. Our problem is not legal gun ownership, it's release of career criminals.

Guns are here to stay. The number of gun owners in America is commonly reported as 60 million, but the real number is closer to double that. With a gun in hand, an untrained citizen can act foolishly brave and reckless, resulting in tragic accidents. With training from the experts and meeting the five criteria, guns save lives.

The following combined NRA and law enforcement efforts would be in the best interest of American gun owners.

Law enforcement training conditions police officers through concentration and discipline to be certain before they open fire. The core result of shoot/no-shoot training is a split-second slowdown of the instinct to open fire, which results in reduced accidental shootings of innocent people.

This same high standard of training in firearms *should be required* for citizens to receive licenses to carry concealed weapons and *should be available* for citizens who keep loaded firearms in their homes for protection. This type of training might have prevented an accidental shooting on November 8, 1994, in Louisiana. A fourteen-year-old girl was at home with a friend when her parents returned home. Expecting to come home to an empty house and sensing someone was there, the father drew his gun. The house was dark and the daughter jumped out of the closet and shouted, "Boo!" Her father, startled, frightened, and thinking his daughter was at a friend's house, immediately fired and killed her. Her last words in his arms were, "I love you, Daddy."

Most firearms experts are within the ranks of the NRA

and law enforcement. A curriculum for citizens that matches the standards for law enforcement should be developed through the combined expertise and resources of these two groups. The NRA and law enforcement could together further decrease the number of tragic accidents with guns.

If such an effort happens, it will depend largely on first separating politics from guns on both sides, then, bringing together law enforcement and the NRA in the most skillful and disciplined firearms training known today, the shoot/no-shoot program. Shoot/no-shoot prepares men and women with the mind-set crucial to making a split-second life-or-death decision with a gun.

2. THE CELLULAR WAVE

Up to 90 percent of the violent crime cases associated with driving a car (outside of the drive-bys) that I saw in twenty years as a cop could probably have been avoided if the motorist had had a cellular phone. When Kristen Dale sat on Interstate 5 for three and a half hours, a cellular phone would probably have prevented her being raped, because she would not have been stranded—she could have called for help. A big issue for teenaged girls and women is the frustration and anxiety they feel while stranded. It's so high that they fight their instincts and accept a ride.

Unlike any other protection measure available, a cellular phone immediately notifies family members and authorities that help is needed and allows the caller to pinpoint where it's needed—nothing is left to chance.

When You Are Not in Your Car

You're taking a walk with your spouse through the park at dusk. The only thing different from normal is that you now have a cellular phone in your pocket. You see some shady-looking characters lurking, or a cruising car. You're not sure, but they look like they're sizing you up. The bad feeling in your gut is growing. The very act of initiating a cellular-phone call while staring at them can give them the impression that you may be calling authorities, giving their location, possibly even physical descriptions and license numbers, and that you're not worth the risk. I predict that cel phones are destined to be as significant a crime deterrent for men and women on foot as they already are for stranded motorists.

Family Outings

Many parents are now carrying their cellular phones not just in cars and on business trips, but also while hunting, fishing, camping, and picnicking. I think of the many cases in which families were brutalized and raped by one or more campsite intruders. A cel phone would not have prevented the attack, but it would have brought medical and law enforcement assistance fast. Not only that, an immediate description of vehicles, attackers, license plates, to law enforcement will make apprehending the criminals more likely.

A Special Group with a Special Need

Teenagers may be the group most in need of cel phones. They're the most mobile, they're out more often, and later at night, and often in potentially dangerous areas. They also think they're invulnerable and usually don't understand the risks. Cel phones can provide a last-chance way of backing out of trouble that they may have gotten themselves into. For example, a girl suddenly realizes that she doesn't want to be driving out to her date's family vacation house on a lake. If he won't change his mind, her choices are to get out on a dark, lonely road or to go along with him. A cellular phone gives her a third choice.

Helping Others

A cellular phone is the best current means of intervening in crimes against others, and even for yourself. It allows you to notify authorities immediately from a safe distance. You don't have to run and find a nearby phone. In many big cities, a responding police officer can be on the scene in sixty to ninety seconds, so that in the time a bystander spends looking for a phone, the owner of a cel phone can already have law enforcement on the way. I've said in many ways in this book, at crime scenes time works against the victim.

An additional advantage to cel phones is that callers can stay at the scene and give police dispatchers accurate descriptions of landmarks and businesses, even if the area is unfamiliar to them. Knowledgeable local police officers can deduce the exact spot from such descriptions. People who don't know the area and who have to leave the scene to phone for help not only take more time looking for a phone but also frequently give wrong locations or directions. I've been on those calls frantically trying to sort out wrong directions knowing the people needing us needed us minutes ago.

On the Road

In all countries, many highways have long, lonely stretches. It's on desolate highways like these that highway robbery, abduction of families, and rape of women are frequently initiated through the ruse of a phony disabled car, often with a woman as a decoy by the car. I'm not opposed to helping a family stranded in the middle of a freeway when it's daytime and you're on a reasonably well-traveled roadway close to a city. Take them to get gas or to the nearest open business where they can wait for help to come.

But in a desolate area, it's another ball game, and I urge you to resist the tug at your heart to stop and physically help (push the car, change a tire) any stranded motorist when apparently there's no one else around. The decoy ruse plays on your best impulses to help the vulnerable, so that you stop close by and get out. Then the men in the nearby brush or in the car make their rush to overpower you. A cellular phone allows you to call for help without endangering yourself.

Beyond the highway ruses used to get to you, if you or a loved one is stranded, a cel phone is crucial. It reduces the wait, the anxiety—and most important, the risk. In a worth-every-cent way, it changes the odds when you're on the road and stranded.

3. COMMUNITY POLICING

Rana Sampson, founder of Community Policing Associates, is a consultant on community and problem-oriented policing for police agencies and communities around the country. A former National Institute of Justice Fellow, White House Fellow, and police officer in New York City, Ms. Sampson holds a law degree from Harvard and a BA from Columbia. She notes:

> Community policing is a partnership forged between citizens, the police, and municipal service providers and others to tackle crime, fear, and disorder in our communities. Characterized by police-community collaboration and problem-solving, it is based on twenty years of research into

police effectiveness and evolved out of a recognition that police needed to do things differently if they were to make a significant impact on crime and other problems they're asked to handle.

In the past, police waited until crimes occurred and then chased the bad guys. If no crook was caught, they took a report. This reactive model for crime intervention provided too little too late; many citizens and police officers became dissatisfied with it. Today, police are being trained to analyze crime problems in a more sophisticated way. They look for patterns and target repeat offenders. The result is a better focus on understanding why certain places in our communities are crime-prone.

In one Florida community, a rash of robberies made residents wary of outdoor activity. Rather than hoping to come across the crooks through ineffective random patrols, the local police examined robbery data. They found that over 50 percent of the robberies were at convenience stores. Of the forty-seven stores, forty-five had been robbed at least twice, some as many as fourteen times. After careful study, the police identified significant differences between the stores that were robbed and those that weren't. The stores that weren't robbed had better lighting in the parking lot, a clear view of clerks, and minimal-cash-on-hand policies. The most significant difference was that robbers tended to avoid convenience stores with two clerks on duty in late-night hours. After implementing the police department's recommendations, the city experienced a 70 percent decrease in convenience-store robberies from the previous year.

In other communities, citizens are highly active in community-policing anticrime efforts. The police cannot fight crime alone and are now willing to acknowledge that creating a safe place to live is everyone's responsibility. On one block in Philadelphia, mothers banded together to form a pots-and-pans brigade to disrupt street-corner drug dealing. In Portland, Oregon, police sponsor training for landlords and apartment managers to help them understand how to rid their property of illegal activity, including drug activity. In San

Diego, merchants, with the help of the police, sought temporary restraining orders against prostitutes who were hailing clients in front of their stores.

In some communities, businessmen look for creative solutions to annoying and recurring crime problems. Grocery store owners, at the suggestion of the police, are playing classical music to dissuade youthful loiterers from hanging out in their parking lots. Owners of some pay phones on corners where drug dealing is prevalent are modifying the phones so that only outgoing calls can be made; users and dealers cannot be called back to set up drug deals, thus dampening dealer profits. And in communities all over the country, residents are using hundred-year-old, dormant nuisance laws to abate drug houses, brothels, and loud party houses in their neighborhoods and gang activity.

Community policing relies on problem-solving as its key component and represents a sea change in how police do their work, a welcome change for both police and communities.

In 1994, Richmond, Virginia, woke up to one of the worst murder rates in the United States, 149 homicides for a city of 200,000. That's stratosphere high—San Diego averages 150 homicides per year and has a population of 1,200,000.

Richmond attacked the problem as a community—they called it Operation Full Alert. It involved almost every crime-suppression idea of recent years: police strike forces in "hot spots," roadblocks, bicycle patrols, citizen patrols, curfews, pay phone restrictions, arresting truants, mentoring, boot camps, specialized courts to keep everything moving fast. Richmond's goal is a 25 percent decline—they're not there yet, but the crime increases have stopped. In all types of crimes, Richmond is finally experiencing declines. However, not everyone is happy with Richmond's zero tolerance. The local and national officers of the ACLU plan to challenge the measures as too extreme.

From my twenty years of experience in law enforcement,

it is clear that law enforcement and community members know who their local criminals, gang members, and drug dealers are. But they're often stopped from taking effective action by federal courts and laws that protect the individual's civil liberties at the expense of the community's needs and rights to protect families. Police officers must show reasonable cause even to detain a gang member just to talk to him, let alone check him for an illegal weapon.

Over and over, communities have tried to suppress local crime, only to have their efforts stopped by one individual unhappy about interference with unlimited civil liberties. In 1994, for example, a gang-ridden, drug-infested Chicago housing project was stopped from taking tough, rights-intrusive, hard-line measures to protect their homes and families from gang warfare when a civil liberties attorney defended one gang member's right to come and go as he pleased. The rights of the children in that project came in second. Many children are exposed to violence and twenty-four-hour-a-day fear. As one teacher said, "When our children return to the projects and are exposed to violence, we can forget about any homework being done." What does that bode for their future? And what about our society's future when our most important resource sees more violence and feels more fear than anything else in their lives?

Community policing, and when necessary, hard-line policing, is the answer to control the currently out-of-control crime in most cities. Without it, we will experience the crime-wave predictions by 2005, predictions echoed by the experts in our best educational institutions, Department of Justice officials, and even the president and Republican candidates opposing him. Unfortunately, they cannot agree on what to do.

The preceding three ways to a safer future are long-term (a few years). The next three ways are needed immediately.

Three Immediate Needs

If we and our leaders are serious about stopping skyrocketing random, senseless, and explosive violence, our first priority must be getting guns, gangs, and recidivists off the streets. Forty percent (average) of murders in all cities of 100,000 or more are committed by guns in the pockets of warring and thrill-seeking gang members or recidivists—the career criminals committing up to 80 percent of all violent crimes. A large percentage of gang members are also recidivists, which makes them double the threat to the rest of us.

Many gang members/recidivists in jails awaiting trial communicate to their partners on the outside who the witnesses against them are.

In May 1995, a Miami drug dealer and gang member was in custody, awaiting trial. He was made aware of a doctor willing to testify against him. Federal officials say that within weeks, the doctor was gunned down with a silencer-equipped pistol in front of a Miami restaurant. That same month in Los Angeles, two women who had agreed to testify against a gang member and drug dealer were gunned down in separate attacks, in what investigators call a "silencing of witnesses."

September 26, 1995, Boston, Massachusetts: Paul McLaughlin, a state prosecutor on an antigang task force, was shot to death entering his car by a teenager wearing a hooded jacket. Police say, "It appears to be an assassination." It's not the first murder of a gang prosecutor; four others have been assassinated since 1980.

"A line has been crossed," said Robert L. Ullman, formerly

head of the Criminal Division of the U.S. Attorney's Office in Boston, ". . . an execution-style slaying of a prosecutor used to happen only in Colombia . . . are we far off from that?"

A few days after the McLaughlin execution in Boston, Mike Runnel, a district attorney leading a gang crackdown in New Mexico, had his office torched.

In the 1920s, organized crime usually bought off witnesses, police, and government officials; now our street gangs just kill them off.

Lt. Sergio Robleto, LAPD homicide detective and supervisor, was blunt in a recent interview *(Los Angeles Times)*: ". . . never seen the ferocity of attempts to kill witnesses. . . . In our bureau alone, we had to evacuate and relocate thirty-nine witnesses and their families, due to death threats by gangs." When asked, "How many witnesses are killed?" Lieutenant Robleto said, "It's too high, too negative. If I released that information, we would drive them [witnesses] underground."

❐ _____

1. GUNS OFF THE STREETS

To stop drive-by shootings and lethal gang wars, we must start by getting illegal guns off the streets. This can't be done without police officers taking guns away from gang members, because gang members don't volunteer to give up their weapons—not even in gun buy-back programs. Gang-bangers who live by and with illegal guns do not exchange them for concert tickets. Police must have the authority to stop 'n' frisk known and suspected gang members and search their cars. That may mean restricting individual rights currently considered sacrosanct, in order to enforce laws already on the books against carrying illegal weapons. Stop 'n' frisk is nothing more than a temporary restriction of freedom for gang-bangers known to police to curtail a problem fatal to all of us.

Allowing police to look for guns and stop emerging gangs is critically important. Eight hundred American cities have documented gang problems. In many cities, as you've read, close to half of all homicides are caused by gang members killing each other and bystanders.

By the time kids have joined a gang and are carrying guns, they are beyond the control of their parents (often a single mom) and school counselors. If a kid isn't stopped fast by a power greater than his gang (like a toughened-up criminal justice system), odds are he will likely become a murderer or a murder victim.

Right now, there are twenty thousand gun-control laws on the books in cities and states throughout the United States. More laws will not stop illegal guns on the streets.

Intervention by law enforcement, backed up by the community, in stopping and frisking known gang members for illegal guns and drugs will reduce random and violent crime. It will also turn some kids around, but it's got to be a community and police team effort.

In one Midwestern town, residents were fearful for their children and angry about gunfire in the streets. One citizen was killed in a gun fight between gang members. The community, outraged by the violence, wanted action. They put a hard-liner into office as marshal, whose first move was to get guns off the streets. It was a bold move, stepping on individual rights, but backed by active community support. Street violence practically disappeared in Wichita 120 years ago with Wyatt Earp as marshal.

One major difference in towns and cities, then and now, is that then they had the authority within their community to enact decisions based on their community's needs. Now, when communities team up with their local police departments, they have the will but no real power to act on their own behalf without concurrence from the various arms of the federal government. Wichita and other towns were able to clean up their communities in the 1800s because they had the will and the authority to police themselves.

We keep hearing that crime in America is too complex for simple solutions. In my experience in law enforcement, every complex problem has been worsened with complex solutions. Consistent, direct, and forceful works against criminals.

After a six-month trial of a community-backed police stop 'n' frisk crackdown in 1994 on known gang members, Kansas City enjoyed a 50 percent decrease in gang-related crimes. The Department of Justice hailed the crackdown as one that might work in other violence-plagued cities. Might? But, the decrease didn't last. As soon as the six-month special efforts ended, gun crimes went back up.

New York City police initiated a plummeting violent-crime rate in what they call "high-crime blocks" with stop 'n' frisk concentration for even minor infractions. New York City cops on the beat evaluated the results simply with, "Gang-bangers are now leaving their guns at home." That's a beginning.

In August 1995, the *Los Angeles Times* ran a question-naire: Should L.A. try "hot spot" stop 'n' frisk policing?

Gary Greenebaum, western regional director of the American Jewish Committee, answered the question best: "The model from New York has a lot of potential . . . but, the community must be aware that it's going to happen, because surprises put people on the defensive."

Nowhere is a crackdown on guns illegally carried more important than in our schools. The Department of Justice estimates that 125,000 kids take guns to school every school day—fifteen years ago, that estimate was less than 1,000. Thirteen kids (on the average) die every day from guns— up from one per day.

> **S**pecific policing based on a citizen and police concurrence on their communities' particular needs is the future of both successful law enforcement and suppression of crime. Federal laws that blanket us all in the same way stop communities from correcting their "hot spot" problems. For example, local stop 'n' frisk police action is usually immediately challenged in a federal court. Communities need relief from federal restrictions aimed at sameness in every community — Kalispell, Montana (I used to live there), experiences vastly different problems from Los Angeles.

A selective stop 'n' frisk police action is no more draconian than sobriety checkpoints.

A new police officer's handheld camera is planned for late 1996 that will enable beat cops to scan a suspected pedestrian for guns, explosives, and drugs. Massachusetts-based Millitech Corp. developed the camera and says the scan can see through all the baggy clothing and coats a person can wear.

It's not a dangerous move for a community to authorize the local police department to come down hard on known criminals and emerging gang members. But, the community needs to be in on the planning and review of such a program, and when it is to be terminated. Every community can and will solve its crime problems without direction from Washington, D.C.–based federal agencies or federal courts because a community's citizens and cops bring up their families there.

"The dynamic you are trying to work on with community policing is giving people a sense of valid control over their neighborhood," said Frank Hartman of Harvard University's Kennedy School of Government.

Of course, there is an understandable concern by some citizens that some community-policing movements might become vigilante movements. Vigilante movements are as dangerous to innocent people as the criminals are. Vigilante action is not the answer, it's not acceptable, and most important, it's not the issue when community and police team together.

2. GANGS

Are there really so many gangs and gang members in communities to justify the draconian move of cutting back on certain civil liberties, in return for greater security and safety? From the April 25, 1995, *Wall Street Journal* series on gangs:

Is No Place Safe Anymore?

"In 1980, 179 cities reported problems with street gangs. In 1995, 800 cities have documented gang problems," Malcolm Klein, director of the Social Science Research Institute at the University of Southern California, reports. "There are currently 4,000, give or take a few, gangs in the United States, with more than a half million members known to police officials." He cautions that this is a conservative number because it doesn't take into account the youngest gang members. In many cities, more than half of all homicides involve gang members killing each other and innocent bystanders during random gang wars and drive-by shootings.

Malcolm Klein is right, his research estimate is conservative. Police gang specialists keeping a daily pulse on individual gangs and numbers of members find far more than half a million gang members nationwide. Chicago police sergeant Robert Stasch (quoted in the Associated Press) reported that the Folk Nation gang, a combination of three separate gangs and strong in Chicago, has an estimated half million members itself nationwide.

Los Angeles police officer and gang specialist Stuart Guidry advises that Los Angeles County is home to approximately 150,000 gang members, with the various factions of the Crips and Bloods being the dominant forces.

Keep this bottom line in mind as you read the next set of figures and summations of sociologists and criminologists: most of the youth crime now and in the future will be the work of gang members.

Tod Klear, professor of criminology at Rutgers University, says, "The past's and the future's most violent group of criminals in America are the fifteen-to-twenty-nine-year-old age group—the average age of gang members."

In the years studied, the fifteen-to-twenty-nine-year-olds represented 24 percent of the U.S. population, but less than 1 percent of that age group actually commit the violent crimes.

- 1969   329 violent crimes were committed per 100,000 in the 15-to-29-year-old group
- 1989   663 violent crimes were committed per 100,000 in the 15-to-29-year-old group (double)
- 1994   1,200 violent crimes were committed per 100,000 in the 15-to-29-year-old group (double again)

The first time, it took twenty years for youth violence to double. The second time, five years.

"We had better buckle our seat belts," says James Fox, dean of the College of Criminal Justice at Northeastern University (quoted earlier). ". . . Murderers are getting younger. Teens are more dangerous than adults. They are least deterrable."

Alfred Blumstein, sociologist at Carnegie-Mellon University, gives the two reasons for the explosion in juvenile violence: ". . . drugs, especially crack, and the proliferation of guns in the hands of young people on the street. If you're a gang member and/or dealing and using drugs on the streets, you have to carry a gun."

With almost complete unison, sociologists and criminologists predict that, unless society makes drastic changes now, by the year 2005 we will experience another crime wave of unprecedented proportions. Because the young-adult malefactors of that time will be even more violent than teenagers now for two reasons. First, they won't have been addicted to crack as teenagers—they will have been addicted to crack since birth, because their mothers were crack users. Second, a large percentage will join gangs because of their older brothers and local heroes—the pressure on a young boy to join is tremendous.

The bottom line: Getting gangs off the streets requires our society to concentrate the community-policing approach on a crackdown on illegal trafficking and possession of guns and drugs. Focusing on just those two criminal violations alone will break the back of street gangs.

3. THE RECIDIVISTS

Less than 1 percent of our population is ruining the peace and safety of our country: the career criminals who rape, kill, and rob the rest of us. Violent career criminals represent less than 10 percent of the total U.S. criminal population. Police know who they are, they have photos of them, names and addresses, too. Recidivist criminals in America commit 75 percent to 80 percent of all crimes, including violent crimes.

It's possible that we could read this headline in every one of our cities' newspapers tomorrow morning:

Recidivists Jailed at End of Day
Crime Dropped 75% Overnight

But, neither you nor I will see this headline until we focus on the heart of our overall criminal justice system failure: recidivism. It's dooming our society; it's our biggest threat and the reason we have such a horrible and extended rise in violence.

The problem is not that recidivism is a new phenomenon or that our society is the only place on earth with the problem. It's simply, we're the country with the worst record of continually releasing prisoners.

Ninety-six percent of prison inmates overall have prior convictions for serious and violent crimes prior to finally ending up in prison. An example:

• 45% have three or more convictions
• 19% have four or more convictions
• 6.7% have eleven or more convictions

In other words, more than 90 percent of prisoners are behind bars because they're dangerous.

If and when criminals finally get to prison, they don't serve long sentences. Average time served:

• Murder . . . 7 to 9 years
• Rape . . . 3 to 5 years
• Robbery . . . 2 to 4 years

When they get out, 70 percent return to crime within the first twelve months and are eventually apprehended within thirty-six months. It's crazy. In thirty years of habitual release of career criminals believed to be rehabilitated, America's criminal recidivism rate climbed to 70 percent, and yet the debate of why in thirty years we have had an overall crime increase of 550 percent continues.

In just one state, California, an average of thirty-two thousand prisoners are paroled each year, after serving less than half of their sentence. Of that thirty-two thousand, over three thousand are rapists, sex perverts, and child molesters—another two thousand are convicted killers.

It gets worse; of the recidivists we apprehend "doing it again," only 49 percent are returned to prison. One reason is limited space in prisons nationwide. The other 51 percent are given "just one more chance."

For whatever psychological reason, rehabilitation and reeducation have not worked to stop violent criminals. For whatever reason, parole has not worked to stop violent criminals.

Perhaps the most infamous recidivist killing was in New York: Winston Moseley stalked and murdered three women in 1964—his third victim was Kitty Genovese. He petitioned the court in August of 1995 for a new trial based on cruel punishment. Winston claimed, "The suffering of my victims was a one-minute affair, but for me, it's been forever."

Less known but similar to all recidivists is Reginald McFadden, a Pennsylvania paroled murderer, who murdered again within three months of his release, a Long Island woman. Then raped and battered another woman in South Nyack, New York. He said at his sentencing, "Sentence me to a thousand years. It won't make any difference."

My personal worst recidivist case—the one that made me angriest—involved a child molester and killer. Twice convicted, twice paroled, he abducted little six-year-old Manuel Garcia from the sidewalk in front of his home while Manuel played alone on his three-wheeler, then molested the boy, then slit his throat and cut off his genitals. His parole papers read in part (like many others), "believed to be emotionally prepared to control any further criminal impulses."

Forget "three strikes" for any violent crime. The only criminal justice that works against recidivism is punishment that is consistent, direct, and forceful. Make it "one strike" in this way! If you commit any crime that seriously injures or kills a human being or use a weapon in the commission of any crime, injury or not, it's life in prison for you. The two key life-in-prison issues should be injuring a human and using a weapon. No exceptions. No excuses. No paroles.

The End of Recidivism?

No society has ever prevented the evil ones within its midst from committing violence. But, some societies have done so much better than others in stopping (once arrested) their evil ones from repeating their violence.

America is one of the most advanced nations and the most powerful, yet, we seem powerless against the 1 percent of our people who repeatedly murder, rape, and rob us— and molest our children. Only a few things, if permitted to continue, can eventually undermine and destroy a society—recidivism is one of them.

Epilogue

THE FACTS ON THE COST OF CRIME

The hue and cry that a "one-strike" system will not work because "we don't have enough cops," "it would cost too much," "the courts will clog up" . . . is all hollow.

Not Enough Cops?

If arresting a recidivist meant putting him away for good, we have more than enough cops. Taking one recidivist off the streets averts an average of 187 small and large crimes per year (DOJ, 1985). The bottom line: One city taking one hundred recidivists off the streets permanently eliminates approximately 18,700 crimes in that city in one year. Instead of a continuing increase of fear and violence unprecedented in America's history, we could in four years of zero tolerance undo thirty years of failed tolerance.

Too Much in Prison Costs?

It costs less to keep recidivists in prison than to release them. Maintaining a man (or woman) in prison costs between $18,000 and $25,000 per year. The variation depends on the level of security. If one thousand recidivists were never released to victimize us again, our costs would be approximately $25 million per year. (If I had the authority, I could cut those costs.) So, how do we save money by not releasing them? The answer is in the costs of their repeat crimes. The bottom line: One recidivist, released, commits an average of 187 crimes per year. The cost to society is not only in human suffering, but it's also $430,000 per year per recidivist in property loss, damage to private and government institutions, increased law enforcement, private security, courts, local jails, private hospitalizations and medical costs, insurance costs for loss and fire damage, fire departments, and the list goes on. This recidivism cost to society is based on a Department of Justice study in the mid eighties. The study concluded with this sentence: "The cost per year to operate our nation's prisons is one-tenth of the cost of crime to society."

What does recidivism mean to your family's safety? The revolving door has costs both in human suffering and the tax dollars spent to keep it revolving.

Clogged Courts? The courts are currently clogged for one simple reason: the recidivists are repeatedly back in court. Just how clogged are courts with recidivists and how much does prosecuting them all over again cost?

San Diego, CA   In September 1995, 75% of all cases were recidivists; 51% of the district attorney's budget was utilized to prosecute recidivists again.

Buffalo, NY   In December 1995, 74% of all cases were recidivists; 60% of the district attorney's budget was utilized to prosecute recidivists again.

The bottom line: If recidivists were not released, our courts would not be clogged, our communities could save a lot of money, we would live in less fear—the emotional and physical suffering of people could be cut 75 percent.

Every president since Lyndon Johnson has had his Get-Tough Crime Bill (according to the Department of Justice, a dozen or more big and small bills since 1964). With all the new laws, hundreds of millions of dollars spent, crime has still skyrocketed 550 percent for one simple reason: we avoided the number one problem, we avoided the tough decision: recidivism. We don't need another crime bill, we didn't need the last one, we only need to get tough on recidivists in a permanent way. Consistent, direct, and forceful is the only effective combatant against career criminals.

We can stop this madness: youth violence, gangs controlling whole communities, gunfights in open daylight in some neighborhoods. But, only if we're willing to put aside personal and political agendas (it's damning that crime has been a political football for as long as I've been eligible to vote) and first concentrate on the three immediate needs for safety: guns, gangs, and recidivists off the streets.

Our only impediment will be, are we yet fed up enough to make the effort it takes? Bill Clinton said as a presidential candidate in 1992, very succinctly, "The definition of crazy is wanting a change without having to change."

My criminal justice bottom line: A man who intentionally and repeatedly injures fellow human beings should lose all rights upon conviction (including constitutional rights, except those providing for basic health, sustenance, shelter, and freedom from physical abuse) and not get them back until full time is served. Is that radical? Is it fair? Is there support for such a bold departure from our present dealings with recidivists? The answer is simple: depends on whom you ask, friends of criminal rights defense or friends of crime victims.

WE'RE AT THE FORK IN THE ROAD

For our nation, it's either cease the thirty-year debate and political tough talk and actually get tough with a zero tolerance for any criminal injuring a human being or using a weapon in any crime—justice should demand punish ment . . .

OR

Give in, as some are already advocating with declarations such as:

"Three strikes is too expensive."

"It's not civilized to lock people up for life."

"Our focus must never shift from rehabilitation."

"The disparity in race, age, and localities is unfair."

For our families, it's a simpler decision with less debate, but the stakes are higher. Either we acknowledge the sometimes depressing and always ugly facts about violent criminals and act with family members before something happens against a loved one . . .

OR

Denying our fears as unnecessary and imagined, believing ignorance is bliss, do nothing and hope random violence doesn't strike us. Which I earlier referred to as the hope-and-luck defense.

If you're fed up with random and senseless crime, if you're shocked by the realities of the cases you've read in this book, if you want to make a potentially lifesaving difference for your family and your friends at work, you need to exercise only one quality: leadership. That's the quality with which all change begins, be it in a government, corporation, or in your home.

Earlier in the book, I spoke of crime-scene leadership: shouting orders and directions to loved ones and fellow workers when the crime is going down. That level of leadership doesn't just happen. It begins ahead of time when men and women plan against the worst so that they will be prepared to lead.

Leading your family or valued employees in learning how to protect themselves and each other is as fundamental to caring about them as care can get.

Your first move is to break the old habit of putting it off until something happens and lead now. Interrupt routines and discuss how to help each other in case the lives of family and friends are at stake. This book is purposely arranged so you can use it as a progressive series of teaching steps: from replacing old habits and myths, to training your survival instincts through mind-setting, to teaching children, to deciding if a gun is right or wrong for your family.

Remember what Bob Rogers said after his family was attacked: "We learned the toughest part of a crisis is the decision-making."

Lead your family and friends in how to break through fear and make split-second survival decisions. They're crucial because as a parent, friend, employer, you get one chance to help another before random violence might strike them. At crime scenes, people are on their own and get no second chances or time-outs to decide what to do.

Your leadership will be the spark for your family, friends, and employees to learn how to protect themselves and later lead their families and friends in how to survive random violence. I ask of you to see in yourself the person who must begin it all. Many of you who do will look back someday (I'm certain) on a crisis loved ones or friends survived and will quietly know your initial leadership contributed to their ability to pull through and give themselves their best chance.

Thank you,
Kathy and Dona,
Ed and Marcia McClain